Here I Stand

Edd Doerr

Rocinante Press
Silver Spring, MD

Potts Publishing

For Herenia

Published 2006 for Rocinante Press by Potts Publishing

ISBN: 0-9785704-1-3

Inquiries should be addressed to:

Rocinante Press
Box 6656
Silver Spring, MD 20916
Telephone: 301-260-2988
FAX: 301-260-2989
email: arlinc@verizon.net

Potts Publishing
PO Box 746
Roseville, CA 95661-0746

Printed in the United States of America

Table of Contents

Preface

Hier stehe ich. Ich kann nicht anders.
Also sprach Martin Luther.

"Here I stand. I can do no other." Martin Luther's proclamation a half millenium ago is the best title I could think of for this book. Although not expansive enough to be called a "summing up," it nonetheless encapsulates my thinking on the topics with which I have been involved for well over half of my life.

Here you will find an address I gave in 2005 in New York, a chapter I contributed to a book, an article reprinted from the Americans for Religious Liberty journal, an essay on the necessity of cooperation to further common goals, testimony at a congressional hearing, a couple of poems that relate to the other material in this book , and a hundred letters to the editor that have been published over the last two years in a variety of publications, and other material. (Let me add that the letters pertaining to my professional work were generally signed with my title of president of Americans for Religious Liberty, while those dealing with views outside this realm were strictly personal.)

As this book contains my fourth collection of letters to editors, it should be obvious that I find this medium a very useful one for trying to influence public opinion. One letter seen by tens of thousands of people may be more significant than a book with only a handful of readers. I would like to encourage readers to follow this example.

Lest I be thought limited in my interests, I should add that life would be incomplete without music, poetry, and literature. I've published some 350 poems, some fiction--an example of which may be found as Appendix III--and have been immersed in music as performer and listener for nearly all of my life.

I must add that anything I may have accomplished over the years is due largely to the fact that I have been standing on the shoulders of giants too numerous even to begin to list.

Acknowledgements

I am grateful to my wife Herenia and my daughter Helena for their invaluable help; to my long-time friends and colleagues Teri Grimwood, who has processed most of what I have written over a quarter-century and serves as a Jane-of-all-trades, and Al Menendez, a walking, talking encyclopedia and fellow scribe; and the innumerable men and women who have generously supported Americans for Religious Liberty these many years.

Edd Doerr
November, 2006

Is Government in America Becoming Faith-Based?

Today marks the end of the war in Europe 60 years ago. It would be appropriate for me, then, to read an important document that few have actually seen. It is dated 7 May 1945 at 0410 hours and comes from the Supreme Head-quarters of the Allied Expeditionary Forces in Europe. I quote:

> A representative of the German High Command signed the unconditional surrender of all German land, sea, and air forces in Europe to the Allied Expeditionary Forces and si-multaneously to the Soviet High Command at zero one four one hours Central European Time, seven May, under which all forces will cease active operations at zero zero zero one baker, nine May.
>
> Effective immediately all offensive operations by Allied Expeditionary Forces will cease and troops will remain in present positions. Moves involved in occupational duties will continue. Due to difficulties of communication there may be some delay in similar orders reaching enemy troops so full defensive precautions will be taken.
>
> All informed down to and including divisions, tactical air commands and groups, base sections, and equivalent. No release will be made to the [press] pending an announcement by the heads of the three governments.
>
> Signed: Eisenhower

At the end of the message are the initials of the Army clerk who typed the communication ending hostilities – "WAS." That's my friend Warren Allen Smith, and Warren is here in the audience today.

An address to the New York Society for Ethical Culture, May 8, 2005.

It is a distinct honor to be here today. It was in this very building a quarter century ago that my good friend, Ed Ericson, then senior leader of this society, led in the formation of the Center for Moral Democracy. At the same time Rabbi Sherwin Wine, the founder of Humanistic Judaism, led in the development of a similar organization in Michigan, Voice of Reason. Both Ed and Sherwin recognized the dangers to our liberties posed by the rise of televangelist Jerry Falwell's so-called Moral Majority and other forces on the religious radical right.

In early 1982, Ed and Sherwin arranged to merge the two organizations into what is now Americans for Religious Liberty. I was honored to be asked to head the organization. In its nearly quarter-century of work, ARL has won court battles (such as *Lamont v. Wood*, in the Second Circuit here in New York early in the Bush I administration), published 90 newsletters and more books in the field than any other organization, and worked closely with other groups to further the cause of church-state separation.

Our subject today may appear at first glance to be rather narrow, but as philosopher Ernst Cassirer observed, "To be is to be related." As we shall see, probably all of the concerns that we share are related, and, in a special sense, related to today's topic.

These concerns, about which we could talk endlessly, include the following, in no particular order:

Preemptive war. Regime change. Genocide. Imperialism and neo-colonialism. The growing gap between the global North and South. Indifference to suffering, poverty, and misery around the world and in our own land. The worldwide HIV/AIDS crisis.

Global warning, deforestation, desertification, overpopulation, addictive overconsumption, environmental degradation and pollution, increasingly rapid exhaustion of nonrenewable resources such as fossil fuels, increasing stress on renewable resources such as fisheries and topsoil and fresh water. Shrinking biodiversity.

Erosion of civil liberties and women's rights. Racism and ethnocentrism. Homophobia. Social fragmentation. The growing gap between rich and poor in this country. Political corruption. Declining citizen participation. The dumbing down of the media and the population. Inadequate funding of public education and health care. The shame of the largest prison population in the world. Increasing government secrecy. Consolidation of ultraconservative control of politics and media. The increasing misuse of religion for political purposes. [This reminds me of the play, "Stop the World, I Want to Get Off."]

We could go on, but you get the idea. So let's turn our attention to the growing threats to church-state separation and how they relate to all of the concerns just listed. There are three aspects to be examined.

One: The propaganda war against church-state separation; the attacks on liberal or progressive politicians, media, and academics; the demonization of "secular humanism," "secularism," and a "culture of relativity," which the new pope, Benedict XVI, has denounced; and any deviation from fundamentalist views on religion, education, sex, and "traditional values," whatever that means.

Two: The specific socio-political agenda of the religious radical right and its secular allies.

Three: The fact that all the effort directed to dealing with Items One and Two seriously distracts attention from working to solve the real social justice and other problems listed earlier.

The propaganda war: Major media have been dumbed down to the point where citizens have to work hard to know what is going on in the nation and the world (that is, if they really care to know). The *New York Times* and *The Nation* reach far too few people. Now we are facing new attacks on public broadcasting with insinuations that NPR and PBS are too "liberal." There are nearly 2,000 radio and TV stations owned by religious outfits and nearly all of them saturate their programming with evangelical and fundamentalist messages, many of them political, reaching an estimated audience of 141 million people. [That's more than read a recent letter of mine in the *New York Times*.] Far right evangelical broadcaster James Dobson reaches millions every day, as do Pat Robertson, Jerry Falwell, D. James Kennedy, and their myriad imitators. Fundamentalist Tim LaHaye, who is several cards short of a full deck, has sold over 60 million copies of his hack "left behind" novels. There are more "Christian" bookstores and bookracks in supermarkets than there are gas stations. Secretive outfits like the Fr. John Hardin Apostolate in Chicago are training cadres of people to flood newspapers and magazines with fundamentalist messages in letters to editors. In April Senate Majority Leader Bill Frist had David Barton, a notorious Orwellian "selective manipulator of history," lead a private tour of the capitol to present his comically distorted view of our nation's history. And the two main organs of conservative opinion, *The Weekly Standard* and *National Review*, both support the positions of the fundamentalists, referred to by some as the "American Taliban."

Well, enough of that. Before proceeding with the religious right agenda, we might take an all too brief glance at our history. Fundamentalists make much of religious references in the Declaration of Independence. Yes, they are there, but let's recall that in 1776 the ragtag forces of our divided country faced the strongest army and navy in the world, the forces of an empire that asserted the "divine right" of kings. How better to counter this idea than with the notion of the "divine rights" of the people. Fundamentalists call attention to the Declaration's reference to a Creator endowing people with inalienable rights. But why did nobody think of that until 1776? And why has the Creator historically not endowed most people, especially women and minorities, with these rights? Let's face it, the Declaration was essentially a propaganda document,

inspired in part by Tom Paine, designed to rally our divided American population to support independence. It's also true that the document encapsulated
important political ideas that are as relevant now as then.

But to move on. The Constitution mentions religion only in forbidding
religious tests for public office and mandatory oaths of office. The Bill of Rights,
adopted shortly thereafter, barred any government action "respecting an establishment of religion, or prohibiting the free exercise thereof." In 1802 Jefferson,
with the concurrence of his attorney general, declared that the First Amendment "erected a wall of separation between church and state." As early as 1879
the Supreme Court held that Jefferson's interpretation was correct.

Meanwhile, nearly all of the states followed Virginia's example and included the idea of church-state separation in their constitutions. It is interesting to note that the constitution of the Commonwealth of Puerto Rico, adopted
in 1952 and approved by Congress, specifies that "There shall be complete
separation of church and state." Meanwhile, also, the Fourteenth Amendment,
approved after the Civil War, made the Bill of Rights applicable to state and
local government.

Beginning at its first opportunity in 1947, the Supreme Court unanimously
affirmed Jefferson's interpretation of the First Amendment, though subsequent
rulings have tended to weaken it. Finally, we might note something the religious
right would rather not be reminded of, that in 1797 President John Adams and
the Senate approved our treaty with Tripoli that declared that "the government
of the United States of America is not in any sense founded on the Christian
religion."

I might mention, by the way, that one of the best books on this subject, *The
Separation of Church and State: Writings on a Fundamental Freedom by
America's Founders*, was published in 2004 by Beacon Press. The editor is
Forrest Church, minister of All Souls Unitarian Church here in New York.

We are now ready to look at the specific agenda of the religious right, in no
particular order.

School Vouchers and Their Analogues: Conservatives have for a great
many years sought to get tax support for private faith-based schools. If suc-
cessful, this campaign would decimate our already underfunded public schools
[a particularly serious problem here in New York State]. It would force everyone
through taxes to support private schools that specialize in sectarian indoctrination and practice forms of selectivity and discrimination that would be intolerable in public institutions. Our society would become ever more fragmented
along religious, ideological, class, ethnic, and other lines. Educational costs
would go up, as former Gov. Rockefeller's Fleischmann Commission concluded
many years ago, while overall educational quality would decline. As private
schools are generally hostile to unions, teaching would become an even less
remunerative and desirable profession than it is now.

Many of you will remember the 1967 constitutional referendum here in New York State. Cardinal Spellman and his friends sought to remove Article XI, Section 3 from the state constitution, the section banning tax aid to faith-based schools. New York voters defeated that attempt 72% to 28%. That referendum was the subject of my first book, *The Conspiracy that Failed*, in 1968.

Since the New York referendum there have been 24 similar statewide referenda from coast to coast between 1970 and 2004. On average vouchers or their analogs were defeated two to one.

Wisconsin and Ohio passed voucher plans in recent years because lawmakers were too afraid to submit the issue to the voters and their state supreme courts failed to apply their own state constitutions. In 2002 the Supreme Court approved Ohio's voucher plan with twisted logic that would make an ambulance chaser blush. The same has occurred in Gov. Jeb Bush's Florida, but that state's supreme court is likely to deep six it.

Charitable Choice: For over a century public support has gone to faith-based charities, but generally with safeguards to prohibit discrimination and proselytizing. (An exception to this rule is Roman Catholic hospitals, which control as many as 20% of all hospital beds, and which generally decline to provide important reproductive health services such as morning-after contraception, abortion, tubal ligations, and vasectomies.) President Bush the Lesser, however, is seeking to buy religious votes, African American and Latino and white, by expanding charitable choice and eliminating the barriers to discrimination and proselytizing. As I pointed out in *The New York Times* on May 2, 2001, Bush's charitable choice plan will "create a growing proliferation of unregulated, unaccountable charities of uncertain efficacy competing for scraps of a shrinking public pie." In addition, "It would violate Madison's 1785 warning that using 'religion as an engine of civil policy' would be 'an unhallowed perversion of the means of salvation'." We are seeing abundant evidence of that.

Religion in Public Schools: Both the Constitution and the pluralistic nature of our society demand that our public schools be religiously neutral. The Supreme Court has been clear on this, especially with the school prayer rulings of 1962 and 1963. Fundamentalists have squawked about this for over 40 years but have never, so far, been able to get a constitutional majority in Congress to approve a prayer amendment, thanks largely to the fact that mainstream religious leaders, including such key figures as Catholic priest and former congressman Robert Drinan, agreed that public schools have no business meddling with religion.

Although the Supreme Court in 1987 held that fundamentalist creationism has no place in public school science classes, the religious right is gathering strength to continue their efforts, most recently in Kansas at this very moment.

Another problem that has never been adequately addressed is what I have termed "the invasion of the soul snatchers." Hundreds if not thousands of fundamentalist proselytizers – from such groups as Young Life, Campus Life, Campus Crusade for Christ, Fellowship of Christian Athletes, Jerry Johnston Ministries, and local fundamentalist churches – have been operating with impunity in public schools across the nation for many years.

Finally, there is the problem of teaching "about" religion in public schools. As a former high school history and government teacher, I agree with the Supreme Court that public schools may try to alleviate ignorance about religion. The problem is that there is no agreement as to precisely what should be taught and at what grade levels; there are very few if any teachers trained, qualified, and certified to teach about religion; and there are few if any suitable textbooks. The difficulties of teaching about religion are so numerous and serious that few public schools and teachers want to try.

[Incidentally, the topics that I am discussing today are covered more thoroughly and extensively in my chapter in the new book, *Toward a New Political Humanism*, edited by Barry Seidman and Neil Murphy, just published by Prometheus Books. My chapter is included in this book; see page 15.]

Reproductive Rights: The right to use contraception was not completely nailed down until the early 1970s, and the constitutional right to choose to terminate a problem pregnancy was not acknowledged until *Roe v. Wade* in 1973. The Supreme Court did not "create" the right; it acknowledged a right that already existed. While the right to choose in *Roe* was based on the Fourteenth Amendment due process right to privacy, it is really much more than that. It should be protected by the Thirteenth Amendment ban on "involuntary servitude," on the seldom-used Ninth Amendment, and on the First Amendment's religion clauses. After all, if the law imposes on women a sectarian view of when personhood begins the establishment clause is violated; if a woman's freedom of conscience is interfered with, the "free exercise" clause is violated.

Regarding a fertilized egg, embryo, or fetus as a person is an idea without any credible backing from the Jewish and Christian scriptures, and even if it did, with no scientific backing. As was pointed out to the Supreme Court in 1988 in *Webster v. Reproductive Health Services* in an *amicus curiae* brief I organized that was signed by twelve Nobel laureates and 155 other scientists, the functions associated with human personhood are not possible until the cerebral cortex is sufficiently developed to permit consciousness, some time after 28 to 32 weeks of gestation.

But the "personhood at conception" idea promulgated by the Vatican and the fundamentalists is really just a cover for the real motive behind the antichoice movement, which is the maintenance of historic male dominance over women.

And not only does the anti-choice movement push hard to make reproductive health care services less and less accessible, especially to young and poor women and those who live in the political "red" states, but the Reagan and Bush I and II administrations blocked U.S. aid to overseas family planning agencies if they so much as approve of abortion. Indeed, Bush the Lesser, against the recommendation of his own advisers, blocked $34 million that Congress had approved for the United Nations Population Fund for two years in a row. As a result of these anti-choice policies, many thousands of women and children die, the abortion rate increases, and the population problem gets worse. [Thirty years ago President Nixon ordered a report on the effects of overpopulation on U.S. security interests. The National Security Study Memorandum 200 report, endorsed by President Ford, was quite similar to the Programme of Action presented by President Clinton at the 1994 Cairo Population Conference. The NSSM 200 report, having been marked classified, was buried for nearly 20 years. Had that not happened, we could have made substantial progress in dealing with population and environmental problems, and might even had headed off the Rwanda massacre in the early 1990s.]

To tie things up, it is obvious that the religious right and its allies, oblivious to the social justice injunctions of the religions they profess, are in the process of making over government at all levels in America into a faith-based operation. At this point we should mention the current controversy over the filibuster. It does not take rocket science to recognize that the 55 Republicans in the Senate represent less than half of the U.S. population. So the filibuster may be all that stands between us and permanent single-party rule. This talibanization of our country will not only greatly shrink the liberties we have come to take for granted but will also disenfranchise many millions of us. And as I said earlier, the success of this trend will make it difficult if not impossible to address the real problems of our country and our planet. And time is running out. Of course, I have no wish to deny the various brands of fundamentalism their right to live and think as they please, but we will all suffer if their drive to political ascendancy succeeds.

What to Do: As individuals we need to tackle as many of these issues as we can. We can volunteer time and effort and money, each according to our individual situation. We can support, in line with our resources and our particular interests, those organizations that are addressing these issues, such as Americans for Religious Liberty (founded in this building), the American Civil Liberties Union (which this society played a role in founding), People for the American Way, the Interfaith Alliance, this society's social justice activities, the Religious Coalition for Reproductive Choice (which the American Ethical Union helped to found), NARAL, and other groups too numerous to list.

We must recognize that we in this hall are not alone. Vast numbers of moderate, liberal, and progressive Catholics, Protestants, Jews, and others share many of our values. We need to promote intergroup cooperation whenever and wherever possible.

Back in the 1960s, here in New York, Leo Pfeffer, Florence Flast, and others formed the Committee for Public Education and Religious Liberty (PEARL). In the 1970s PEARL became a national organization. Unfortunately, always short of cash, it faded away two or three years ago. Now we need a similar but bigger and more comprehensive organization in New York, New Jersey, Connecticut, and every other state. A good model to emulate would be the Texas Freedom Network (www.tfn.org), which has been doing terrific work in a state that, as one wag put it, is missing its village idiot.

If evil triumphs, it will be largely because good people did not do enough to stop it. And as Kahlil Gibran put it, "Let passion fill your sails, but let reason be your rudder."

The Importance of Church-State Separation

During almost fifteen centuries has the legal establishment of Christianity been on trial. What have been its fruits? More or less, in all places, pride and indolence in the clergy; ignorance and servility in laity; in both, superstition, bigotry, and persecution.
— James Madison, *Memorial and Remonstrance*

Separation of church and state, of religion and government, is probably the United States' most important single contribution to political theory and practice. That separation, though generally supported by most Americans over the past two centuries, is nonetheless in serious jeopardy today. In order to understand the current threats to separation and to promote strategies for defending that vitally important principle, it is necessary to take a deep and broad historical perspective, however condensed it must be for the purposes of a chapter of reasonable length. This chapter, then, will sketch the origins of the principle, trace its development from theory to practice, summarize the very real current threats (in no special order), and offer suggestions for action.

Background

Throughout history and throughout the world, religion and government have been closely intertwined. In some cultures there was/is no distinction between these two powerful forces. Some Islamic and even some Christian fundamentalists insist today that there should be no separation. While in Western history, of which the United States is a product, religion and government came to be distinguished or distinguishable in theory, in actual fact they were/ are linked in a variety of ways and to varying degrees.

This article is reprinted, by permission, from *Toward a New Political Humanism*, edited by Barry F. Seidman and Neil J. Murphy, Prometheus Books, 59 John Glenn Drive, Amherst, NY 14228-2197. © 2004 by Barry F. Seidman and Neil J. Murphy.

For example, some Western countries provide tax support to religious schools; some still have established churches (in the United Kingdom the monarch is titular head of the Church of England, a fact that resulted in the curious anomaly of the governor of Maryland enjoying the same titular status, even when the governor was Jewish); some still have compulsory or semicompulsory church taxes.

Established churches were the rule when the first Europeans – British, French, Dutch, German, Swedish, and even Jewish – settled the east coast of North America. Although many of these Europeans came to America for freedom of religion, they brought the European established church tradition with them. By the end of the seventeenth century, the Anglican (Episcopal) Church was established in all colonies from Maryland to Georgia, while Puritan Congregationalism was established in all the New England colonies except Rhode Island.

By the start of the American Revolution, the colonies had become fairly pluralistic and included Anglicans, Congregationalists, Roman Catholics, Baptists, Methodists, Presbyterians, Lutherans, Quakers, Unitarians, and Jews. This pluralism set the stage for the development of church-state separation. The idea was first articulated by Roger Williams, the Rhode Island maverick, who seems to have influenced John Locke, and finally flowered under Thomas Jefferson and James Madison in Virginia during and immediately after the Revolution. By 1786, thanks in part to Madison's brilliant 1785 pamphlet, *Memorial and Remonstrance against Religious Assessments,*[1] the church-state separation principle become law in Virginia, setting the pattern that the other states would sooner or later follow.

In 1787, the United States Constitution created the country's present form of government. Significantly, it implies the principle of church-state separation by granting to the national government no authority whatever to meddle with religion. Indeed, the only mentions of religion are in Article VI, prohibiting religious tests for public office and mandatory oaths of office.

The new Constitution would be ratified, but only after Madison and politicians in Virginia and elsewhere promised to add a Bill of Rights to it. Indeed, Madison's good friend Jefferson, then ambassador to France, stressed the importance of such an action. The first Congress, meeting in 1789, drafted twelve amendments, ten of which were approved and ratified. After much discussion, the two houses of Congress settled on the following wording for what became the First Amendment: "Congress shall make no law respecting an establishment of religion, or prohibiting the free exercise thereof; . . ."

In recent years, there has been much debate over whether the First Amendment supports the "separationist" side, as most Supreme Court justices have held since the first major case on the issue in 1947, or the "accommodationist" or "nonpreferentialist" side, represented today by Chief Justice William Rehnquist and Justices Antonin Scalia and Clarence Thomas and on Patrick

Henry's losing side in Virginia in the 1780s. An examination of the debates over the text of the amendment shows that the separationists, following Jefferson and Madison, won.[2]

The "separation of church and state" metaphor was popularized by President Jefferson's January 1, 1802, letter to the Baptist Association of Danbury, Connecticut, a letter that Jefferson cleared with Attorney General Levi Lincoln. Jefferson wrote, "I contemplate with sovereign reverence that act of the whole American people which declared that their legislature should 'make no law respecting an establishment of religion, or prohibiting the free exercise thereof,' thus building a wall of separation between church and state."[3]

In 1879, the US Supreme Court noted that "Jefferson's use of the term 'wall of separation between church and state' may be accepted almost as an authoritative declaration of the scope and effect of the amendment thus secured."[4]

Not until 1947, however, did the Supreme Court actually apply the separation principle. The decision in *Everson v. Board of Education* put it this way:

> The "establishment of religion" clause of the First Amendment means at least this: Neither a state nor the Federal Government can set up a church. Neither can pass laws which aid one religion, aid all religions, or prefer one religion to another. Neither can force nor influence a person to go to or remain away from church against his will or force him to profess a belief or disbelief in any religion. No person can be punished for entertaining or professing religious beliefs or disbeliefs, for church attendance or non-attendance. No tax in any amount, large or small, can be levied to support any religious activities or institutions, whatever they may be called, or whatever form they may adopt to teach or practice religion. Neither a state nor the Federal Government can, openly or secretly, participate in the affairs of any religious organizations or groups and vice versa. In the words of Jefferson, the clause against establishment of religion by law was intended to "erect a wall of separation between church and state."[5]

Backtracking a bit, Jefferson acknowledged in his 1802 letter to the Danbury Baptists that the First Amendment applied only to the federal government, not to state and local governments. It was only in the aftermath of the Civil War that Congress approved and the states ratified the Fourteenth Amendment, which was intended to make the Bill of Rights applicable to state and local governments.[6]

Meanwhile, following the example of Virginia, the rest of the states adopted the separation principle.[7] It is significant that the last two states admitted to the Union in 1959, Alaska and Hawaii, included the separation principle in their constitutions.[8] Perhaps even more significant is the fact that in 1952 Congress considered and approved the Constitution of the Commonwealth of Puerto

Rico, which not only reiterates the language of the First Amendment but also adds these words, "There shall be complete separation of church and state."[9]

Church-state separation, then, is, as they say, as American as apple pie. Nonetheless, hurricane winds are blowing that would topple Jefferson's wall.

The Threats Today

Storm warnings need to be posted for all to see. The threats to the wall are very real and very serious. Led by sectarian special interests and by televangelists such as Pat Robertson, Jerry Falwell, and numerous others, the Religious Right has virtually taken over one of our major political parties on the national and state level, a great many politicians feel that they are beholden to the Religious Right, the media have been shifting steadily to the right, and the Supreme Court itself has drifted away from the strong separationist position it held for so long after 1947.

A complete catalogue of all the threats to the "wall of separation," great and small, would stretch this chapter to intolerable length, so it will concentrate on the most serious threats: tax aid to faith-based schools and charities, dealing with religion in public schools, and reproductive freedom of conscience.

School Vouchers and Their Analogues

Since around 1960, there has been a rising chorus of demands for tuition vouchers, tuition tax credits (sometimes referred to as "tax code vouchers"), and other forms of federal and/or state tax aid for nonpublic schools. About 90 percent of US kindergarten through twelfth-grade students attend public schools in some fifteen thousand local school districts. Of the remaining 10 percent, about 90 percent attend Catholic, fundamentalist, Quaker, Jewish, Adventist, Muslim, and other "faith-based" schools. The religious demands originally came mainly from the Catholic-school sector, which claimed about 90 percent of the enrollment in faith-based schools in 1965, about 5.5 million students. By 2004, for reasons to be discussed later, Catholic school enrollment had plunged to about 2.5 million. Since 1965, then, total nonpublic school enrollment has declined both proportionally and in absolute numbers. The rise in evangelical or fundamentalist schools, which began with the desegregation of public schools, has not equaled the decline in Catholic schools.[10]

Nonreligious support for vouchers and their analogues started with economist Milton Friedman, soon joined by others of like mind. The usual rationale given for vouchers, and similar programs, is that parents should be able to choose where to educate their children and that competition among schools will somehow improve all schools. The literature on this subject is too vast even for a short bibliography, so this discussion will be as comprehensive as possible in as little space as possible.[11]

Parental choice in schooling is largely a chimera. A 1998 US Department of Education study found that there are not all that many seats available in nonpublic schools, that almost invariably nonpublic schools practice forms of discrimination in admissions that would be intolerable in public schools and which would not be abandoned, and that very few faith-based schools would be willing to exempt tax-supported voucher students from denominational religious instruction.[12] The report, for reasons unknown, neglected to mention that faith-based schools frequently use faith criteria in hiring and firing teachers. Further, faith-based schools tend to be pervasively sectarian and often ideology-oriented.[13] Thus the pervasively sectarian nature of the vast majority of nonpublic schools and their admissions and hiring policies would tend to homogenize student bodies by religion and perhaps less often by social class, ethnicity, ability level, and other ways. A large-scale voucher plan, then, would tend to fragment school populations and communities along religious and other lines to a far greater degree than at present. As for competition improving all schools, it should be obvious that Catholic, Jewish, Muslim, Lutheran, and Protestant fundamentalist schools do not really compete with one another.

Nor does the evidence support the claims that voucher plans, whether public or private, improve all schools, whether in the United States or in other countries with some form of "school choice." In the two cities that already have voucher plans as of 2004, Milwaukee and Cleveland, state laws do not permit meaningful evaluation of the supposed benefits of tax support for nonpublic schools.

So much for the case for school vouchers or their analogues. The case against vouchers is so much stronger that in the twenty-five statewide referendum elections on vouchers or their analogues from coast to coast between 1967 and 2000, vouchers were rejected by an average margin of two to one, most recently in California and Michigan in 2000.[14]

Tax aid to nonpublic schools through vouchers, at anything close to current per capita spending on public schools, would necessarily either increase taxes or decrease support for public education. In an era of severe strain on federal and state budgets, we are not likely to see the necessary tax hikes. Moreover, it is already well known that US public schools are seriously underfunded and that within virtually every state, funding for public education has long been inequitably distributed. And just to repair or replace broken-down public school buildings throughout the country, according to one federal study, would cost far more than the $87 billion that President George W. Bush requested in mid-2003 for the reconstruction of Iraq.

And the preceding does not factor in the $2 billion or so in federal and state funds going to faith-based schools annually, the huge cost of simply transporting students to a growing proliferation of nonpublic schools, or the fact that voucher costs would impact adversely on rural and smaller communities. In

Pennsylvania, for example, the state's 501 public school districts are required by state law to transport students up to ten miles beyond school district boundaries, which has already imposed a heavy burden on many districts.

We might remember, too, that the Fleishman Report to New York governor Nelson Rockefeller more than thirty years ago concluded that it would be cheaper for the state to take all nonpublic school students into public schools than for the state to support the nonpublic schools.[15]

Economics aside, vouchers would force taxpayers to support the forms of discrimination and religious indoctrination common in nonpublic schools, the sort of thing that Jefferson labeled "sinful and tyrannical."

We come at last to the question of constitutionality. Unfortunately, during the last decade or so, the Supreme Court has moved away from the fairly strict separationism of 1947. In June 2002, the Court even held that the Cleveland school voucher plan does not violate the First Amendment, a ruling that defied logic, common sense, and the facts.[16] So, as civil libertarians learned in recent years, the Supreme Court is no longer a reliable defender of the fundamental liberties of citizens.

Fortunately, public opinion and most state constitutions continue to maintain a wall of separation although the Wisconsin and Ohio courts have not seen fit to do so. However, a new effort by voucher advocates is under way to remove state constitutional barriers to vouchers, tied to a grossly exaggerated claim that state constitutional barriers to vouchers are the product of nineteenth-century anti-Catholic bigotry.[17] It is to be hoped that this effort will not succeed, as in 1972 the Supreme Court turned back an effort to do the same thing in Missouri.[18] The charge of anti-Catholic bigotry is refuted by the fact that in 1986 voters in 50 percent Catholic Massachusetts voted 70 percent to 30 percent to defeat an attempt to change the state constitution to allow vouchers.[19] According to exit polls in California and Michigan in 2000, Catholic voters rejected vouchers by about the same two-to-one margin as non-Catholics.

It is worth mentioning that the decline in Catholic school enrollment from half of American Catholic children in 1965 to less than 20 percent in 2004 is due to several factors: the election of a Catholic, pro-separation president in 1960; the Supreme Court's 1962-63 rulings against the essentially Protestant practice of school-sponsored prayer and Bible reading in public schools; the liberalization of the Catholic Church under Pope John XXIII and Vatican Council II, 1962-65; negative reaction to the 1968 papal encyclical condemning contraception; and Catholic achievement of proportionate representation in politics.

Another ace in the hole in the struggle over vouchers may well be a seldom-mentioned 1973 Supreme Court ruling that held that even textbook loans "are a form of tangible financial assistance benefiting the schools themselves" and that "a state's constitutional obligation requires it to steer clear not only of operating the old dual system of racially segregated schools but also of giving significant aid to institutions that practice racial or *other invidious discrimination*" (emphasis mine).[20]

The last chapters in the battle over school vouchers have yet to be written.

Charitable Choice

There is no doubt that religion-related charities have done enormous good in this country and elsewhere. Sometimes this is done entirely with voluntarily donated funds but more recently with at least partial public funding. Until 2003, however, religion-related charities receiving tax aid were required by civil rights laws to avoid discrimination in hiring and providing services and to avoid proselytizing.

However, beginning with President George W. Bush, efforts are being made to eliminate the nondiscrimination requirements, either by law or executive order, and to allow these charities to promote religion itself if that is their wish, as in drug or alcohol counseling or prisoner rehabilitation. As I have pointed out elsewhere, this new movement, if not checked, will create a growing proliferation of "unregulated, unaccountable charities of uncertain efficiency competing for scraps of a shrinking public pie" as well as "violating Madison's 1785 warning that using 'religion as an engine of civil policy' would be 'an unhallowed perversion of the means of salvation'."[21]

A colleague and I have summarized the objections to the new movement, evidently introduced to President Bush by Texas fundamentalist writer Marvin Olasky, as follows:

> President Bush's "charitable choice" expansion would clearly violate the church-state separation principle; it would have government pay religious groups for what they have always done on their own; religious minorities could suffer discrimination under the plan; it could radicalize the delivery of services and threaten the religious freedom of recipients; participating churches could lose their "prophetic edge" and become domesticated branches of the civil bureaucracy; government will be forced to choose among competing religious programs, with the most politically connected getting more than their "fair share"; nonsectarian and secular programs could become second-class and underfunded; religious programs are not necessarily superior to secular services; the promoters of "charitable choice" often use the idea for partisan political advantage; President Bush has used dishonest tactics and appeals to religious prejudice to win support for his program.[22]

These objections could be expanded upon, but that would require a great deal of space. Suffice it to note that a study of the deleterious effects of charitable choice in Texas under then-governor George W. Bush was released by the Texas Freedom Network late in 2002.[23]

Religion in Public Schools

Given the astonishing and growing pluralism of religion and other lifestances in the United States and the constitutional requirement of separation of church and state, it should be obvious that the public schools serving American children must be religiously neutral. The courts have dealt with some of the issues involving public schools,[24] but not all, and with fifteen thousand locally responsible school districts in the country, there is no accurate way of surveying all the possible problems and their permutations. So we will have to make do with a hopefully not too superficial overview.

Contrary to popular opinion, government-sponsored prayer and Bible reading, essentially nineteenth-century Protestant affairs, were never universal. They were confined mainly to the East Coast and the South. The practice was halted by the Supreme Court in 1962 and 1963 rulings.[25] Despite tremendous exertions by the Religious Right, all subsequent attempts to amend the Constitution to authorize school-sponsored devotions failed to obtain the necessary two-thirds vote of either house of Congress, thanks in large measure to opposition to such amendments by leaders of mainstream religious denominations. Controversies continue, but even a weakened Supreme Court has not shown signs of caving in on this issue.

Controversies still erupt, however, over the teaching of evolution in public school science classes. Despite the fact that in 1987 the Supreme Court ruled that Fundamentalist biblical "creationism" is religion, not science, and therefore has no place in public school science classes,[26] creationists have not given up. They exert every effort, especially in the South, to water down the teaching of evolution or to get public schools to promote the notion of "intelligent design," a modified form of creationism that has no significant scientific support.

On the whole, as most of the witnesses (including this writer) who testified before a mid-1998 hearing before the US Commission on Civil Rights agreed, "the relevant Supreme Court rulings and other developments have pretty much brought public education into line with the religious neutrality required by the First Amendment. . . ."[27] In August 1995, the US Department of Education issued advisory guidelines to all school districts on religious expression in public schools. At the 1998 Civil Rights Commission hearing, Julie Underwood, general counsel for the National School Boards Association, told the hearings that inquiries to the NSBA about what is or is not permitted in public schools declined almost to the vanishing point once the guidelines were published.[28]

The guidelines grew out of a document titled "Religion in the Public Schools: A Joint Statement of Current Law," issued in April 1995 by a broad coalition of thirty-six religious and civil liberties groups. Declaring that the Constitution "permits much private religious activity in and around the public schools and does not turn the schools into religion-free zones," the statement went on to detail what is and is not permissible in the schools.[29]

On July 12, 1995, President Clinton discussed these issues in a major address at – appropriately – James Madison High School in northern Virginia and announced that he was directing the secretary of education, in consultation with the attorney general, to issue advisory guidelines to every public school district in the country. The guidelines were issued in August. In his weekly radio address of May 30, 1998, anticipating the June 4 House debate and vote on the Istook (R-OK) school prayer amendment, President Clinton again addressed the issue and announced that the guidelines, updated slightly, were being reissued and sent to every school district. This effort undoubtedly helped to sway the House to vote down the Istook amendment.

The guidelines, based on fifty years of court rulings (from the 1948 *McCollum* decision to the present), on common sense, and on a healthy respect for American religious diversity, have proved useful to school boards, administrators, teachers, students, parents, and religious leaders. Following is a brief summary:

> *Permitted*: "Purely private religious speech by students"; nondisruptive individual or group prayer, grace before meals, religious literature reading; student speech about religion or anything else, including that intended to persuade, as long as it stops short of harassment; private baccalaureate services; teaching about religion; inclusion by students of religious matter in written or oral assignments where not inappropriate; student distribution of religious literature on the same terms as other material not related to school curricula or activities; some degree of right to excusal from lessons objectionable on religious or conscientious grounds, subject to applicable state laws; off-campus released time or dismissed time for religious instruction; teaching civic values; student-initiated "Equal Access" religious groups of secondary students during noninstructional time.
>
> *Prohibited:* School endorsement of any religious activity or doctrine; coerced participation in religious activity; engaging in or leading student religious activity by teachers, coaches, or officials acting as advisors to student groups; allowing harassment of or religious imposition on "captive audiences"; observing holidays as religious events or promoting such observance; imposing restrictions on religious expression more stringent than those on nonreligious expression; allowing religious instruction by outsiders on school premises during the school day.
>
> *Required:* "Official neutrality regarding religious activity."[30]

In reissuing the guidelines, Secretary of Education Richard Riley urged school districts to use them or to develop their own, preferably in cooperation with parents, teachers, and the "broader community." He recommended that principals, administrators, teachers, schools of education, prospective teachers, parents, and students all become familiar with them.[31] As President Clinton declared in his May 30, 1998, address, "Since we've issued these guidelines, appropriate religious activity has flourished in our schools, and there has apparently been a substantial decline in the contentious argument and litigation that has accompanied this issue for too long." The incoming Bush administration in 2001 reissued the guidelines in a somewhat weakened and confusing form.[32]

As good and useful as the guidelines are, especially the original versions, there remain three areas in which problems continue: proselytizing by adults in public schools, music programs that fall short of the desired neutrality, and teaching appropriately *about* religion.

In addition, conservative evangelists such as Jerry Johnston and Jerry Falwell have described public schools as "mission fields." In communities from coast to coast, proselytizers from well-financed national organizations, such as Campus Crusade and Young Life, and volunteer "youth pastors" from local congregations have operated in public schools for years. They use a variety of techniques: presenting assembly programs featuring "role model" athletes, getting permission from school officials to contact students one-on-one in cafeterias and hallways, volunteering as unpaid teaching aides, and using substance abuse lectures or assemblies to gain access to students. It is not uncommon for these activities to have the approval of local school authorities. Needless to say, these operations tend to take place more often in smaller, more religiously homogeneous communities than in larger, more pluralistic ones.

Religious music in the public school curriculum, in student concerts and theatrical productions, and at graduation ceremonies has long been a thorny issue. As Secretary Riley's 1995 and 1998 guidelines and court rulings have made clear, schools may offer instruction about religion, but they must remain religiously neutral and may not formally celebrate religious special days. What, then, about religious music, which looms large in the history of music?

There should be no objection to the inclusion of religious music in the academic study of music and in vocal and instrumental performances, as long as the pieces are selected primarily for their musical or historical value, as long as the program is not predominantly religious, and as long as the principal purpose and effect of the inclusion is secular. Thus there should be no objection to inclusion in a school production of religious music by Bach or Aaron Copland's arrangement of such nineteenth-century songs as "Simple Gifts" or "Let Us Gather by the River." What constitutes "musical or historical value" is, of course, a matter of judgment and controversy among musicians and scholars, so there can be no simple formula for resolving all conflicts.

Certain activities should clearly be prohibited. Public school choral or instrumental ensembles should not be used to provide music for church services or celebrations, though a school ensemble might perform a secular music program in a church or synagogue as part of that congregation's series of secular concerts open to the public and not held in conjunction with a worship service. Hymns should not be included in graduation ceremonies. Students enrolled in music programs for credit should not be compelled to participate in performances that are not primarily religiously neutral.

As for teaching *about* religion, while one can agree with the Supreme Court that public schools may, and perhaps should, alleviate ignorance in this area in a fair, balanced, objective, neutral, academic way, getting from theory to practice is far from easy. The difficulties should be obvious. Teachers are very seldom adequately trained to teach about religion. There are no really suitable textbooks on the market. Educators and experts on religion are nowhere near agreement on precisely what ought to be taught, how much should be taught and at what grade levels, and whether such material should be integrated into social studies classes, when appropriate, or offered in separate courses, possibly electives. And those who complain most about the relative absence of religion from the curriculum seem to be less interested in neutral academic study than in narrower sectarian teaching. Textbooks and schools tend to slight religion not out of hostility but because of low demand, lack of time (if you add something to the curriculum, what do you take out to make room for it?), lack of suitable materials, and fear of giving offense or generating controversy.

The following questions hint at the complexity of the subject:

- Should teaching about religion deal only with the bright side of it and not with the dark side (religious wars, controversies, bigotry, persecutions, and so on)?
- Should instruction deal only with religions within the United States, or should it include religions throughout the world?
- Should it be critical or uncritical?
- Should all religious traditions be covered or only some?
- Should the teaching deal only with sacred books – and, if so, which ones and which translations?
- How should change and development in all religions be dealt with? To be more specific, should we teach only about the Pilgrims and the first Thanksgiving, or also about the Salem witch trails and the execution of Quakers?
- Should schools mention only the protestant settlers in British North America or also deal with French Catholic missionaries in Canada, Michigan, and Indiana and with the Spanish Catholics and secret Jews in our Southwest?

- Should we mention that Martin Luther King was a Baptist minister but ignore the large number of clergy who defended slavery and then segregation on biblical grounds?
- Should teaching about religion cover such topics as the evolution of Christianity and its divisions, the Crusades, the Inquisition, the religious wars after the Reformation, the long history of anti-Semitism and other forms of murderous bigotry, the role of religion in social and international tensions, the development in the United States of religious liberty and church-state separation, denominations and religions founded in the United States, controversies over women's rights and reproductive rights, or newer religious movements?

The probability that attempts to teach about religion will go horribly wrong should caution public schools to "make haste very slowly" in this area. Perhaps other curricular inadequacies – less controversial ones, such as those in the fields of science, social studies, foreign languages, and world literature – should be remedied before we tackle the thorniest subject of all.

The American landscape has no shortage of houses of worship, which generally include religious education as one of their main functions. Nothing prevents these institutions from providing all the teaching about religion that they might desire.

The late Supreme Court Justice William Brennan summed up the constitutional ideal rather neatly in his concurring opinion in *Abington Township S.D. v. Schempp,* the 1963 school prayer case:

> It is implicit in the history and character of American public education that the public schools serve a uniquely public function: the training of American citizens in an atmosphere free of parochial, divisive, or separatist influence of any sort – an atmosphere in which children may assimilate a heritage common to all American groups and religions. This is a heritage neither theistic nor atheistic, but simply civic and patriotic.[33]

Reproductive Rights

Freedom of conscience and freedom of choice in reproductive matters are often regarded as just "women's issues." They are that, but they are also religious liberty and church-state issues and, beyond that, have a direct bearing on the global problems of overpopulation and sustainable growth. That they are religious liberty and church-state issues is attested to by the existence of the Religious Coalition for Reproductive Choice, founded in 1973, a coming together of forty Catholic, Protestant, Jewish, Unitarian Universalist, and humanist denominations and groups that embrace a wide spectrum of views on reproductive matters but which agree on the importance of reproductive choice as a religious liberty issue. Arrayed on the other side of the question are powerful religious leaders representing the more conservative end of the Catholic, Protestant, and Jewish spectrum.[34] It should also be noted that conservative religious opposition to choice has less to do with theology (the Bible is silent on abortion) than with a patriarchal bent toward male dominance.

The Supreme Court's 1973 ruling in *Roe v. Wade* and *Doe v. Bolton* recognized a constitutional right to privacy that covered not only the right to use contraception but also the right of a woman to choose to terminate a problem pregnancy. *Roe* has so far stood the test of time and public opinion, but the Supreme Court has allowed state legislatures to impose some restrictions on the right to choose, such as waiting periods, mandatory presentation of misinformation to women seeking abortions and burdensome or excessive regulation of reproductive health clinics.

Although the Supreme Court has dealt with reproductive choice as a "constitutional right to privacy" matter, the issue also clearly has to do with "establishment" and "free exercise." Government restriction of choice is tantamount to establishing or preferring one religious perspective over all others, that is, the theological notion that "personhood" begins at conception as opposed to the view that "personhood" begins much later, such as after the cerebral cortex is sufficiently developed to permit the possibility of consciousness or at birth. Governmental restriction on choice also runs counter to "free exercise," which is largely synonymous with freedom of conscience.

As for the relation between reproductive choice and global population/ sustainability, the Reagan, Bush I, and Bush II bans on US aid to overseas reproductive health agencies that might provide abortions or abortion counseling with other than US tax monies represent political cave-ins to sectarian special interests, which exacerbate population/sustainability problems and actually endanger the health and lives of countless women and children in developing countries.

One tragic consequence of conservative religious influence on public policy was what happened to a report titled "Implications of Worldwide Population Growth for US Security and Overseas Interests" ordered by President Nixon and approved in 1974 by President Ford.[35] Had this report not been classified and suppressed for fifteen years, it might have helped prevent the Rwanda massacre in the early 1990s, which it essentially predicted, and allowed the United States and other countries to get a more timely start on dealing with the population/sustainability problem. The report actually anticipated the proposals that the Clinton administration brought to the 1994 UN population conference in Cairo. Another consequence was President George W Bush's withholding of $34 million that Congress had appropriated for the United Nations Population Fund.

What to Do?

Though the preceding discussion is admittedly sketchy and incomplete, it does present a bird's-eye view of a major set of problems. Added to the plate of other concerns of thoughtful citizens in the arena of politics, civil liberties, civil rights, environment, economics, and so forth, we clearly face a concern overload. No one person or group can deal with all of these issues, but each of us, I think, has a moral and social obligation to become involved to the extent of our ability and resources.

We can all participate in the political process, not merely by voting but also by working in and supporting the political organizations and candidates we prefer. We also need to bear in mind that no religious tradition is monolithic. Liberals and progressives in all traditions can, do, and must cooperate in the defense of fundamental liberties, while fundamentalist factions in many traditions work for opposite ends.

We can work in and through – and provide financial support for – the local, state, and national organizations that we consider important. A few of the groups actively dealing with the problems treated in this article are the American Civil Liberties Union, People for the American Way, Americans for Religious Liberty, the Interfaith Alliance, teacher and school administrator organizations, NARAL Pro-Choice America, Planned Parenthood, the Religious Coalition for Reproductive Choice, and the Texas Freedom Network, to name but a few. As the old proverb has it, it is better to light a candle than to curse the darkness.

Notes

1. James Madison, "Memorial and Remonstrance against Religious Assessments," in *The Papers of James Madison,* ed. William T. Hutchinson and William M. E. Rachal (Chicago: University of Chicago Press, [1962]-1991), 8:298-304; "Amendment I (Religion," The Founders' Constitution, http://press-pubs.uchicago.edu/founders/documents/amendI_religions43.html. Also published in its entirety in *Great Quotations on Religious Freedom*, comp. And ed. Albert J. Menendez and Edd Doerr (Amherst, NY: Prometheus Books, 2002), p. 209.

2. Although a whole library has been devoted to this issue, the most concise treatment of it is probably Robert S. Alley's *Public Education and the Public Good* (Silver Spring, MD: Americans for Religious Liberty, 1996), reprinted from Alley's long article in *William and Mary Bill of Rights Journal* 4, no. 1 (Summer 1995).

3. Jefferson to the Baptist Association of Danbury, Connecticut, January 1, 1802, in *Writings* (New York Literary Classics of the US, 1984), p. 510.

4. *Reynolds v. United States*, 98 U.S. 145 at 164.

5. *Everson v. Board of Education*, 330 U.S. 15, 16.

6. Irving Brant, *The Bill of Rights: Its Origin and Meaning* (Indianapolis: Bobbs-Merrill, 1965), pp. 318-43.

7. Edd Doerr and Albert J. Menendez, *Religious Liberty and State Constitutions*

(Amherst, NY: Prometheus Books, 1993).

8. Ibid., pp. 20, 35.

9. Ibid., p. 16.

10. See, for example, Edd Doerr and Albert J. Menendez, *Church Schools and Public Money: The Politics of Parochiaid* (Amherst, NY: Prometheus Books, 1991); and Edd Doerr, Albert J. Menendez, and John M. Swomley, *The Case against School Vouchers* (Amherst, NY: Prometheus Books, 1996).

11. Ibid.

12. U.S. Department of Education, *Barriers, Benefits, and Costs of Using Private Schools to Alleviate Crowding in Public Schools* (Washington, DC: November 3, 1999), cited in Edd Doerr, "Give Us Your Money . . . ," *Phi Delta Kappan* (June 1999).

13. See Albert J. Menendez, *Visions of Reality: What Fundamentalist Schools Teach* (Amherst, NY: Prometheus Books, 1993); Edd Doerr, *Catholic Schools: The Facts* (Amherst, NY: Humanist Press, 2000); Frances R.A. Patterson, *Democracy and Intolerance: Christian School Curricula, School Choice, and Public Policy* (Bloomington, IN: Phi Delta Kappa Educational Foundation, 2003).

14. Albert J. Menendez, "Voters Versus Vouchers: The Forgotten Factor in the Debate," *Americans for Religious Liberty Newsletter* 86, no. 1 (2004).

15. *The New York State Commission on the Quality, Cost, and Financing of Elementary and Secondary Education* (Albany, NY: February 9, 1972), cited in *Church & State* (April 1972).

16. *Zelman v. Simmons-Harris*, 122 S. Ct., at 2460 (2002). The dissenting opinion showed how the majority played word games to dilute the Cleveland program, 96 percent of whose funds went to sectarian schools.

17. See Albert J. Menendez, "Blaming Blaine: A Distortion of History," *Voice of Reason*, no. 2 (2003).

18. *Brusca v. State of Missouri*, 332 F.Supp. 405 US 1050.

19. Albert J. Menendez, "Voters versus Vouchers."

20. *Norwood v. Harrison*, 93 S. Ct. 2804.

21. Edd Doerr, letter to the editor, *New York Times*, May 2, 2001.

22. Albert J. Menendez and Edd Doerr, *The Case against Charitable Choice: Why President Bush's Faith-Based Initiative Is Bad Public Policy* (Silver Spring, MD: Americans for Religious Liberty, 2001).

23. Texas Freedom Network Education Fund, "The Texas Faith-Based Initiative at Five Years: Warning Signs as President Bush Expands Texas-Style Program to National Level," Texas Freedom Network, October 10, 2002, http://www.tfn.org/issues/charitablechoice/report02.html.

24. Perhaps the most useful summary of leading Supreme Court rulings in this area is Robert S. Alley, ed., *The Constitution and Religion: Leading Supreme Court Cases on Church and State* (Amherst, NY: Prometheus Books, 1999).

25. Ibid., pp. 171-93, 195-218, 249-69.

26. Ibid., pp. 219-31.

27. Edd Doerr, "Religion and Public Education," *Phi Delta Kappan* (November 1998): 223-25.

28. Ibid., p. 224.

29. American Civil Liberties Union et al., "Religion in the Public Schools: A Joint Statement of Current Law," April 1995, Religious Liberty, American Civil liberties

Union Freedom Network archives, http://archive.aclu.org/issues/religion/relig7.html.

    30. Doerr "Religion and Public Education," p. 224.

    31. Ibid.

    32. American Civil Liberties Union et al., "Religion in the Public Schools."

    33. *Abington Township S.D. v. Schempp*, 374 U.S. 203, at 224-25.

    34. While there is an abundance of literature on this subject, two useful books are Edd Doerr and James W. Prescott, eds., *Abortion Rights and Fetal "Personhood"* (Centerline Press, 1990), and John M. Swomley, *Compulsory Pregnancy: The War against American Women* (Amherst, NY: Humanist Press, 1999).

    35. Stephen D. Mumford, *The Life and Death of NSSM 200: How the Destruction of Political Will Doomed a U.S. Population Policy* (Raleigh, NC: Center for Research on Population and Security, 1996).

The Bible Goes to School

Considerable attention has been drawn to a textbook produced by the Bible Literacy Project (BLP) in Fairfax, Virginia, for use in teaching about the Bible in public high schools. *The Bible and Its Influence* (BLP Publishing, 2006, 387 pp.) is a lavishly-illustrated, three-and-a-half pound, 9 x 12 inch page size textbook that the BLP reportedly spent five years and $2 million to develop.

While Americans may be the most religious people in the industrialized world, they are also the most religiously illiterate and ignorant. Alleviating ignorance would be a good thing. In ruling unconstitutional school- or state-sponsored or mandated devotional Bible reading in public schools in 1963 in *Abingdon v. Schempp*, the US Supreme Court noted that "It might well be said that one's education is not complete without a study of . . . the history of religion and its relationship to the advancement of civilization. . . . Nothing we have said here indicates that such study of the Bible or of religion, when presented objectively as part of a secular program of education, may not be effected consistently with the First Amendment."

As a former teacher I can say without fear of contradiction that this is far easier said than done. There is no agreement among scholars, educators, or religious leaders as to precisely what should be taught about religion, how much, at which grade levels, whether it should be taught in social studies or language arts courses, whether mandatory or elective, and whether the instruction should be Pollyannishly bland and positive or historically accurate with warts and all. If the kids are going to learn about Dr. Martin Luther King Jr. or antebellum Quaker abolitionists, shouldn't they also learn about clergy who used the Bible to defend slavery and segregation? If the kids learn about the great cathedrals of Europe and the vast amount of religious art, music, and literature, shouldn't they also learn about the religious wars, pogroms, heresy trials, executions of Quakers in colonial Massachusetts?

The Bible and Its Influence appears at first glance to be a good-faith attempt to adhere to the requirement of both the First Amendment and the pluralistic nature of our society that teaching about religion be objective, balanced, and inclusive. The Jewish and Christian scriptures are undeniably significant, one of the most influential sets of writings in Western history, but there is more to alleviating ignorance about religion than simply learning superficially about the Bible.

To its credit the text replaces "BC" (Before Christ) and "AD" (Anno Domini) with the more neutral "BCE" (before the common era) and CE (the common era). The book also contains a comparison of the differences in the ordering of the books of the Hebrew scriptures and those of the Christian "Old Testament," and a list of the Apocrypha in the Catholic and Eastern Orthodox canons but not in the Protestant version, though the text does not attempt to explain why the orderings are different, not an unimportant matter.

Another odd omission: The copyright page indicates that "three translations of the Bible are used in the book," the King James (Protestant) version, the Jewish "Bible" (which Jews prefer to call the Scriptures), and the New Standard Revised Version produced by the National Council of Churches. There is no mention of the Catholic Bible, nor is the Catholic Church represented in the National Council.

The BLP textbook can be read with profit by students and adults of a wide religious spectrum, especially as it dwells largely on the Bible's significant influence on literature, art, rhetoric, and music.

However praiseworthy *The Bible and Its Influence* may be, it has serious shortcomings as a public school text. It does not place the Bible in historical context. It contains no hint that the "earliest" sections of the Hebrew scriptures were written after the "Babylonian captivity"; no reference to the distinction between the Yahwist and Elohist strains in the Hebrew scriptures; no discussion of the contradictions in the Bible or of which parts may be historically more reliable and which are probably myths handed down through oral tradition; virtually no reference to the evolution of Hebrew religious thought or borrowings from other religions and cultures; no attention to "Q" or other sources of the Gospels; no mention of the controversies over what Jesus said or whether things like the utterances in the Sermon on the Mount were delivered in one speech or "assembled" from various sources by the Gospel writers.

Given that all too few students are anywhere near well-grounded in ancient or world history, I must conclude that a student finishing a course using this textbook will have a distorted, truncated, simplistic view of the subject matter. The book makes no reference to the abundant biblical scholarship of the last two centuries.

The Bible does not exist in isolation. The educated person must see how the Bible developed, how the official canon came to be developed, what was going on with real people in the real world during biblical times and during the long centuries after Christianity became the official religion of the Roman Empire, how Christianity won out over its competitors and how it borrowed from them, and what were the effects of the revival of ancient learning transmitted to Europe through Spain by the Arabs, the breakup of the Empire, the Crusades, the Inquisition, the Reformation, the Counter-Reformation, the rise of nation states, colonialism, anti-Semitism, religious wars, the development of religious toleration and freedom and church-state separation.

If public schools cannot present a comprehensive, balanced, fair, inclusive picture of religion in all its complexity, such instruction should not be offered until the student reaches college, though even there few students would likely sign up for an elective course, much less a major or minor. Of course, social studies and language arts as courses cannot avoid dealing with religion at appropriate points, within the restraints imposed by the First Amendment, basic fairness, and our pluralism.

Finally, it is curious that the two "general editors" of the book are a retired publishing executive, Cullen Schippe, and a venture capitalist, Chuck Stetson, whose qualifications to produce this sort of textbook are not to be found. What is to be found, according to one journalist, is that Stetson "has long been active in conservative religious and political causes"; that his father "supported far-right GOP candidates Alan Keyes and Gary Bauer"; that he "is the 'major organizing force' behind the National Bible Association, which . . . promotes the Bible as the path to salvation"; that "Stetson is a disciple of Charles Colson" and that fundamentalist extremist and convicted Watergate conspirator Charles Colson is a strong supporter of the BLP textbook, referring to it "as helping open the door to another 'great awakening' of evangelical religious fervor."

Odd also is the fact that while the book lists two "general editors," nowhere does it name the actual authors, as does every other textbook I've seen. However, the fundamentalist Christian Communications Network revealed last November that among those involved with the BLP are Charles Haynes and Os Guinness, whose 1990 curriculum on religious liberty was analyzed by ARL and found to be seriously deficient as a public school text.

Competing with the BLP textbook is the curriculum produced by the North Carolina-based National Council on Bible Curriculum in Public Schools (NCBCPS), which is claimed to be used in elective courses in over 1,000 high schools in 36 states, though which schools seems to be a carefully guarded secret.

A scathing 42-page analysis of the NCBCPS curriculum by Southern Methodist University biblical scholar Mark A. Chancey, available from the Texas Freedom Network (tfn.org), concludes that "the curriculum advocates a narrow sectarian perspective taught with materials plagued by shoddy research, blatant errors and discredited or poorly cited sources." Chancey concludes that the curriculum is "clearly inappropriate" for public school use. A similar conclusion was reached by Anti-Defamation League director Abraham Foxman, who said that "This wholly inappropriate curriculum crosses the line by teaching fundamentalist Protestant doctrine."

Endorsers of the NCBCPS curriculum include actor Chuck Norris, church-state revisionist David Barton, Phyllis Schlafly's Eagle Forum, Beverley LaHaye's Concerned Women for America, extreme right Rabbi Daniel Lapin, former Senator Jesse Helms, former Representative J.C. Watts, and Pat Robertson's American Center for Law and Justice. Need more be said?

Teaching about religion in public schools, however desirable or well-intentioned, is a very hot potato I have yet to see successfully juggled. Oxford University Press's 17-volume Religion in American Life series is a worthy effort, but its more than 3,000 pages is too much for even four semesters in high school and even then covers only religion in America for the last 500 years and does not deal with the ancient world or the history of Europe, much less the development of religion in the rest of the world.

I believe that the BLP effort's faults outweigh its good points and therefore it should be of higher priority for public schools to improve and expand the teaching of history, science, foreign languages, and world literature, and leave religious education to the university, the home, and the church, synagogue, mosque, or temple, at least until qualified scholars produce properly objective and balanced texts and teachers are adequately trained to deal with this important but extremely complex subject.

Humanism at the Crossroads

> *Two roads diverged in a yellow wood,*
> *And sorry I could not travel both*
> *And be one traveler, . . .*
> . . .
> *I shall be telling this with a sigh*
> *Somewhere ages and ages hence:*
> *Two roads diverged in a wood, and I –*
> *I took the one less traveled by,*
> *And that has made all the difference.*
>   Robert Frost

Humanists, like Frost's traveler, stand at a crossroads. We must choose which road to take, and that will indeed "make all the difference."

As humanists, we have a very long list of concerns. Let me mention some of them, in no particular order:

Preemptive war. Regime change. Genocide. Imperialism and neo-colonialism. The growing gap between the global North and South. Indifference to suffering, poverty, and misery around the world and in our own land. The worldwide HIV/AIDS crisis.

Global warming, deforestation, desertification, over-population, addictive overconsumption, environmental degradation and pollution, increasingly rapid exhaustion of nonrenewable resources such as fossil fuels, increasing stress on renewable resources such as fisheries and top-soil and fresh water. Shrinking biodiversity.

Erosion of civil liberties and women's rights. Racism and ethnocentrism. Homophobia. Social fragmentation. The growing gap between rich and poor in this country. Political corruption. Declining citizen participation. The dumbing down of the media and the population. Inadequate funding of public education and health care. The shame of the largest prison population in the world. Increasing government secrecy. Consolidation of ultraconservative control of politics and media. The increasing misuse of religion for political purposes.

We could go on, but you get the idea. I presented this litany of concerns in an address at the New York Society for Ethical Culture on 8 May 2005 [see page 7]. I also cited Ernst Cassiner's observation that "to be is to be related." What I meant in this context was that all of these concerns are related and, not only that, but also that they cannot be dealt with as long as a coalition of fundamentalist theocrats and their ultraconservative "secular" allies are on the ascendancy, dominating the American political scene, the media, and public discourse. Their propaganda war is primarily devoted to demonizing "secularists" (including mainstream religious folk and organizations) and ceaselessly pushing an agenda that includes privatizing education and social services, obtaining tax support for faith-based schools and charities, undermining the religious neutrality of public education (through injections of government-sponsored devotions, literalist biblical creationism, infiltration of missionaries, and wiping out reproductive freedom of conscience in the not-so-hidden interest of clericalism and perpetuating male dominance.

The following will give a hint at the extent and nature of the Religious Right command of the media.

We are facing new attacks on public broadcasting with insinuations that NPR and PBS are too "liberal." There are nearly 2,000 radio and TV stations owned by religious outfits and nearly all of them saturate their programming with evangelical and fundamentalist messages, many of them political, reaching an estimated audience of 141 million people. [That's over 100 times as many as may have seen a letter of mine in the *New York Times*.] Far right evangelical broadcaster James Dobson reaches millions every day, as do Pat Robertson, Jerry Falwell, D. James Kennedy, and their myriad imitators. Fundamentalist Tim LaHaye, who is several cards short of a full deck, has sold over 60 million copies of his hack "left behind" novels. There are more "Christian" bookstores and bookracks in supermarkets than there are gas stations. Secretive outfits like the Fr. John Hardin Apostolate in Chicago are training cadres of people to flood newspapers and magazines with fundamentalist messages in letters to editors. In April of 2005 Senate Majority Leader Bill Frist had David Barton, a notorious Orwellian "selective manipulator of history," lead a private tour of the capitol to present his comically distorted view of our nation's history. And the two main organs of conservative opinion, *The Weekly Standard* and *National Review*, both support the positions of the fundamentalists, referred to by some as the "American Taliban."

We stand at Frost's crossroads. We have to choose whether to go down the road with vast numbers of people who share our concerns but not necessarily our worldview, or to head down another road with a tiny coterie who are proud to project first and foremost a rather cranky negative image.

Let's look at some appropriate examples. The first is part of a list of "The Ten Top Lies About Church and State," a lengthy address delivered in early April: "Our nation's founders were born-again, Bible-Believing evangelical Christians"; "We don't have a separation of church and state in America because those words are not in the Constitution"; "Church-state separation comes from mid-19th century anti-Catholic bigotry and 20th century secularism"; "The U.S. is a Christian nation"; "Church-state separation was not set up to bar government from aiding all religions on a nonpreferential basis"; "The First Amendment applies only to the federal government, not to the states"; "God has been kicked out of the public schools . . . [and] out of the public square."

Before revealing the identity of the speaker, I'd like to present another example.

During the late summer of 2005, in anticipation of the September 14-16, 2005 UN World Summit in New York City, more than 200 leaders from 37 different countries on all six continents signed a statement urging inclusion in the UN's Millennium Development Goals of support for "universal access to freely chosen reproductive health care services and the human rights noted so eloquently at the 1968 International Conference on Human Rights in Tehran and echoed at the 1994 International Conference on Population and Development in Cairo: The right to determine freely and responsibly the number and spacing of children."

"Promoting reproductive health and rights upholds freedom of thought, conscience, and religion for all members of the human family," the statement added. It also advanced eight specific goals: 1. Eradicate extreme poverty and hunger; 2. Achieve universal primary education; 3. promote gender equality and empower women; 4. Reduce child mortality; 5. Improve maternal health; 6. Combat HIV/AIDS, malaria, and other diseases; 7. Ensure environmental stewardship; 8. Develop a global partnership for development.

Which humanists are responsible for these two expressions of "humanist" thinking? Well . . . .

The first example was from a speech delivered at the Hardin-Simmons University School of Theology in Abilene, Texas, by Brent Walker, executive director of the 70-year-old Washington-based Baptist Joint Committee on Religious Liberty, one of the most effective defenders of church-state separation in the nation's capital. Walker, incidentally, was on a workshop panel that I chaired at the 2003 American Humanist Association conference in Washington.

The second statement was put together by the Washington-based Catholics for a Free Choice. And the largest number of signers were Catholics from around the world, including 43 from Spain and Latin America, plus five dozen mainstream Protestants, two dozen Jews, nine Unitarian Universalists, and a sprinkling of Muslims and Hindus. Most of the signers were clergy or religious leaders of some sort. I was the only identified humanist among the signers, as immediate past president of the AHA.

The point of all this is simply that identified humanists, whether or not their numbers are augmented by identified atheists and "infidels," are not sufficiently numerous to be taken seriously with regard to dealing effectively with the concerns listed at the beginning of this essay. It should be obvious to all but the most obtuse and narrow that effective action to confront the real world threats to our planet, our species, and our cherished liberties will require cooperation among humanist and progressives of every religious persuasion.

For humanists to team up visibly with the identified atheists and infidels, whose most visible interest is being negative toward all religion, is to alienate the vast numbers who share most of our values and who, like us, have nothing but scorn for the Falwells, the Robertsons, the Dobsons, and their ilk.

Let me cite a consequence of humanist taking the second road.

On 19 February 2005 the *San Francisco Chronicle* published a front page interview with a new lobbyist for the Secular Coalition for America, which represents the American Humanist Association and atheist and "infidel" groups.

The story consisted of 37 short paragraphs, 25 of which contain the word "atheist," plus references to "godless," "unbelievers," "atheists [who] aren't 'out yet'," and "Madalyn Murray O'Hair," once dubbed by *Life* magazine as "the most hated woman in America." There was a single mention of the word "humanist" and it came after the word "atheist."

There was nothing in the article about the humanist concerns mentioned in the beginning of this essay. The Secular Coalition appears to be concentrating on defending "atheism," which means getting all worked up over just one item in the long list of things that humanists do not include in their belief or lifestance system.

Should humanists be known primarily for one negative thing or for the great many things they are for? Painting themselves into a corner with people and organizations known almost exclusively for one thing they are against is guaranteed to lead to isolation, irrelevance, and decline. The history of freethought groups in the U.S. bears this out.

Humanists stand at the crossroads and the path they choose will make all the difference.

The U.S. and the Holy See

On a number of occasions I have been privileged to testify at congressional hearings on such topics as tax aid for faith-based schools and judicial appointments.

The following is my oral and written testimony at a February 9, 1984, hearing before a subcommittee of the House appropriations Committee on the subject of "Reprogramming Funds for United States Mission to the Vatican [sic!]."

In the run-up to the 1984 elections President Reagan proposed having the U.S. grant diplomatic recognition to the Holy See, the headquarters of the Roman Catholic Church, which is distinct from Vatican City, a sovereign microstate in Rome created in 1929 in the Lateran Pact between Pope Pius XI and Benito Mussolini.

President Truman had made a similar proposal but it ran into a brick wall of public opposition and was dropped. President Nixon floated a trial balloon through evangelist Billy Graham and it too was blocked by popular opposition.

An obstacle to Mr. Reagan's plan was a law passed by Congress in 1867 prohibiting expenditure of any public funds for a legation in Rome, then the capital of the Papal States, which were incorporated into the Kingdom of Italy in1870, to the displeasure of the Holy See. Congress' 1867 law was a response to widespread negative reactions to serious religious liberty violations by the Papal States and the Catholic Church.

To establish diplomatic relations the Reagan administration had to get Congress to repeal the 1867 law, which it did despite considerable opposition. Then the administration had to have Congress reprogram State Department appropriations to cover an ambassador's salary and expenses. That is the subject of the hearing at which I testified.

The separationist side lost in Congress and in the Supreme Court on grounds of standing and foreign policy considerations. Interestingly, every U.S. ambassador to the Holy See since 1984 has been a Catholic, which would seem to violate the no religious test for public office provision in the Constitution's Article VI.

* * *

My name is Edd Doerr. I represent the Unitarian Universalist Association, the American Ethical Union, the American Humanist Association, the Council for Democratic and Secular Humanism, and Americans for Religious Liberty, the last of which I serve as executive director.

My church affiliation, the Unitarian Universalist Church, has taken a stand at its annual General Assembly of elected delegates. I wrote the resolution which as passed in 1973 on this subject. It was passed with no opposition noticed.

All of the groups that I represent today take a very strong position against either the appointment of any ambassador or the appropriation or reprogramming of any funds to support such an office.

I am impressed by the wide spectrum of opposition to this move on the part of the Administration. It runs from the American Civil Liberties Union on one hand to Senator Jesse Helms on the other. Theologically, from the Unitarian Universalist Association and the American Humanist Association to the National Association of Evangelicals and most religious bodies in between.

The organization for which I work, Americans for Religious Liberty, is an ecumenical organization with Catholic, Jewish, Protestant, Humanist, and other members. We represent the whole spectrum.

I think the gentlemen from the State department who were here earlier might serve us in foreign affairs with some distinction, but they should be a little more truthful with a congressional committee when they appear before it.

They seem unable to distinguish between the Vatican City, which is a small enclave in Rome and the Holy See, which is indistinguishable from the Catholic Church itself.

Of course the President, the executive branch, has most of the prerogative in foreign affairs and in diplomatic relations, but not exclusively. The Senate has to approve nominees to ambassadorships and the entire Congress has to concur in appropriating any funds whatsoever that are used to support that.

There is a possibility that if this move is not stopped by Congress, since the Administration did not see fit to examine it with great care, that it would be tested in court.

However, as a previous witness, a constitutional scholar, mentioned, there might be problems in bringing the litigation, problems of standing, problems of whether they might be regarded as an international political issue and therefore not litigable. [This was exactly what happened when the challenge reached the Supreme Court. I was one of the plaintiffs.]

So it may be that this body, this subcommittee, or the whole Appropriations Committee, or this House may be the only forum in which these constitutional issues are aired, because the courts might not hear them. Our responsibility or the responsibility of both houses of Congress is to look closely at the constitutionality of this move, because the courts may not have that opportunity.

The gentlemen from the State Department seemed to be saying that President Reagan's move is a resumption of relations which we had with the Holy See from 1798 through 1867. That is completely wrong.

The relationships which we had then were with the Papal States, a real country in the middle of Italy, with 160,000 square miles—that is about the size of the state of Maryland, I guess—and a population of three million, abut three quarters of the population of Maryland. That was perfectly legitimate.

If the Republic of Italy today would return the Papal States to the Vatican, and it would set up a state, I wouldn't have any problem with sending them an ambassador. But what the State Department, what the President, is doing, is sending an ambassador not to the Vatican City, which does have sovereignty, but to a church itself. It is an ambassador to the church, and that is precisely what is wrong with it.

I think this move is unconstitutional because it clearly prefers one religion over all others. It unconstitutionally creates the potential, if not the actuality, for entanglement between our government and one church.

As has been pointed out elsewhere, it will exacerbate and create tensions between different faiths in our country. It will create political divisions along religious lines. This was something the Supreme Court has warned us the 1st amendment was intended to prevent.

Something else. The man who wrote the 1st amendment, James Madison, said that—what the President is doing by implication, the civil magistrate is employing religion as an instrument of civil policy. That is what the primary author of the 1st amendment said was wrong. This current President is doing something which the fourth President of the United States said was clearly improper.

The State Department or various people have tended to confuse the President sending an ambassador to the Holy See with sending one to the Court of St. James in London.

Well, our relationships to Queen Elizabeth are of a secular relationship. We are not there because she is a titular head of the church of part of the United Kingdom.

It is also erroneous to equate relations with the Vatican with relations with Israel. Israel is a secular state. We are represented in secular matters with Israel. It has nothing to do with Judaism whatsoever.

One might adduce another example. That is when Cyprus was headed by President Makarios who happened to be a bishop in the Orthodox Church. We had an embassy in Cyprus. It was not to Bishop Makarios as a church official, it was to Bishop Makarios as President of Cyprus. There is a great difference, which the present Administration seems not to take into account.

What the President is doing is, he is conveying to Americans the impression that one faith is better than others. Since this is 1984, it reminds one of the Orwellian dictum that all pigs are equal but some are more equal than others.

This line blurs our really unique American constitutional dividing line between church and state. No other country has this in its constitution. All of the other 107 countries who have embassies in the Vatican have no constitutional separation of church and state, none at all, so we are unique.

If everyone else, as my father used to tell me, runs and jumps in the river, that is no reason for me to go and do so.

If this action is not stopped by the Congress, this violation of the spirit and the letter of the 1st amendment will render the 1st amendment more vulnerable and more weak to other forms of erosion and attack.

I think it is fine that the good offices of churches are used by some countries to settle disputes, such as the dispute between Chile and Argentina over the Beagle Channel.

Fine, those countries are predominantly Catholic countries, and they wanted to find somebody who presumably would be neutral between them to arbitrate the dispute.

Fine. If Norway and Sweden should have a little dispute over a tiny island in the Arctic Ocean, perhaps they would seek some body of Lutheran bishops, since they are both Lutheran countries, to decide the matter, or if Jordan and Saudi Arabia had a quarrel over a little bit of sand someplace, they might go to some Islamic scholars.

I don't see any problem with that, but none of that has to do with our extending diplomatic relations to a church. That is what is wrong.

Since I was involved to a certain extent in the Nigerian civil war of 1967 through 1970, in which the Holy See played an interesting and not too well known part, where if we had diplomatic relations with the Vatican in the late 1960s—how that would have affected our possible involvement in perhaps a second Vietnam in the middle of Africa. We narrowly avoided involvement in that war. What would have happened if we had diplomatic relations with the Vatican?

Lastly, as I think someone else has said and it ought to be reemphasized, the Vatican can make contributions to peace and social justice throughout the world. It doesn't need our recognition to do that. If there is any communication that needs to take place among the religious bodies or between any religious body and our government, it can be done without diplomatic channels.

What the Reagan Administration seems to be saying with this appointment is that the Vatican would withhold information vital to the cause of peace from us because we don't have diplomatic recognition. That is an insult to the head of the Catholic Church for our Administration to even imply that that is what it is doing.

We conclude that it is important that this subcommittee, the Appropriations Committee, the Congress itself, must rectify the error that the Administration has made.

Since the judiciary may not get into the act for purely technical reasons—now, such a constitutional scholar as Leo Pfeffer has pointed out, just because something is not litigable doesn't mean it is not unconstitutional. It may be unconstitutional, but there may be no practical way to get it before the courts, and since we cannot count on the Supreme Court of the United States descending to the stage like the deus ex machina of the old Greek dramas, Congress is going to have to exercise that role.

The ball has been passed to you, and it must be uncomfortable, but the President is the one who passed it to you.

Rep. Carr. Thank you very much, Mr. Doerr.

Rep. O'Brien. Mr. Doerr, let me just tell you my concerns. I think the witnesses have made very eloquent cases, frankly. On principle, I don't find any distinction between envoy and ambassador, if you are dealing with a constitutional issue.

Secondly, you may be right. Maybe this is not wise for the United States, both the Congress and the President, to do this, but it does seem to me that if the Supreme Court believes that it is perfectly okay for us, and I subscribe to the view, to pay a salary to a minister of a particular faith, and that not be found unconstitutional, I find it difficult to suggest that sending an ambassador is.

They aren't exactly parallel cases, I understand that, but I think you are getting into a realm, as I see it, of policy as distinguished from constitutionality.

Mr. Doerr. I don't think so. The Marsh v. Chambers case or Chambers v. Marsh was an interesting one. I think the lower courts were correct. The District Court in the Nebraska case held that the state of Nebraska could not expend any money, any public funds, for a chaplain, but if the members of the Nebraska Senate chose, of their free will, to invite a preacher to pray over them, that was their prerogative, but they couldn't spend any of the taxpayers' money for that.

The Court of Appeals went a little further than that, and the Supreme Court fell back. I think one of the reasons was that there was something waiting in the wings.

As Mr. Dooley said, the Supreme Court follows the election returns. The Chambers case was a good case, but following on its heels in the wings was a case somewhere in the court system by Madalyn Murray O'Hair challenging the congressional chaplains.

If the Court had upheld either of the lower courts in Chambers then it would have had to agree with Madalyn Murray O'Hair on the congressional chaplains, and can you imagine the public furor that would have been directed against the Court?

I think the Court was between a rock and a hard place, and the issue of congressional chaplains is one that is fairly trivial.

I am not sure how many people are present in the morning when the chaplain reads his prayer, but it is not a matter of enormous moment. I think that establishing relations with a church through the White House, through the Administration, is a matter of far more gravity than a chaplain praying before a legislature in the morning when no one is paying attention and most people aren't there.

Rep. Carr. Let me try to get what the remedy is here from your point of view. We were just going over a bit of the legislation.

The law that was passed in November and signed into law November 22, repeals an appropriations bill that was passed in February of 1867. Now, it would appear then that one of two things might happen. An effort might be legislatively mounted by your group and others like you to repeal what was done last year. Another way would be to invite the Appropriations Committee to reinstate the language of the Congress back in 1867.

Do you know whether the groups that have opposed this issue have formulated a strategy?

Mr. Doerr. I do not know, but I don't see any point in arguing about the repeal of the 1867 law. It merely repealed a law on the books that was basically a dead letter.

The Congress, though it did not deliberate this and did not hold hearings, did not take a positive step of allocating any money or of expressing approval for the expenditure of any money for this purpose. It merely removed from existing law a prohibition against something we weren't doing anyway. That is fine. The Congress need not do anything about the repeal of the 1867 law that went through last year.

What I hope we're all asking the Congress to do is simply not reprogram any State Department funds for use for a Vatican embassy. If no funds are allocated for that purpose—and hopefully the Senate would reject the confirmation of an ambassador—then the President would be in a rather awkward position of having established relations and having no way to carry them out, and might then try to find a graceful way to back out of a situation that he shouldn't have gotten himself into in the first place.

The Congress need take no positive action whatsoever. All it has to do is not appropriate or reprogram any funds in response to the State Department request. You don't have to do that. In fact, because there are serious constitutional issues here, which may not be adjudicated, I think Congress needs to look at whether it is appropriate to take any action on the State Department request. I would like to conclude that the House would find this is constitutionally improper and would just simply let the request die.

Rep. Carr. We will be marking up a State Department appropriation sometime this spring. It may be possible that language could be put in that appropriations bill which would essentially be the same as that of 1867.

Mr. Doerr. I am not advocating putting that language into any legislation. I don't think it is at all necessary, just as we don't have any legislation prohibiting relations with Mars or Antarctica. We don't have to prohibit it.

One simply has to not do anything about this. All we are asking, I think, is that the House let this request die, for constitutional reasons.

Rep. Carr. Thank you, Mr. Doerr, for your excellent testimony.

(Written Statement)

Statement to: House Appropriations Committee Subcommittee on Commerce, Justice, State, Judiciary and Related Agencies

Subject: Funding of Embassy to the Holy See

By: Unitarian Universalist Association of Churches
American Ethical Union
American Humanist Association
Council for Democratic and Secular Humanism
Americans for Religious Liberty

Presented by: Edd Doerr, Executive Director, Americans for Religious Liberty, PO Box 6656, Silver Spring, MD 20906

February 9, 1984

Mr. Chairman and Members of the Committee:

The Unitarian Universalist Association, the American Ethical Union, the American Humanist Association, the Council for Democratic and Secular Humanism, and Americans for Religious Liberty are strongly opposed to the appropriation of funds or the reprogramming of existing State Department funds for the operation of a diplomatic mission to the Holy See. Indeed, we oppose the establishment of diplomatic relations with the Holy See. While diplomatic relations are largely the prerogative of the president, Congress shares in this responsibility in that the Senate must confirm diplomatic appointments and both Houses must concur in the allocation of funds for the expenses of diplomatic missions.

The Unitarian Universalist Association, with 175,000 members, is composed of over 1,000 congregations in the U.S. Unitarian Universalism has a long history in our country, going back to the time of the American Revolution. Indeed, the church of the Pilgrims in Plymouth, MA, is a Unitarian Universalist church. The UUA has long supported the constitutional principle of separation of church and state. At its annual General Assembly in 1973 the delegates voted virtually unanimously for a resolution reaffirming support for church-state separation and specifically opposing any sort of diplomatic relations with any church.

The American Ethical Union, the American Humanist Association, and the Council for Democratic and Secular Humanism are national associations of congregations and individuals who strongly support religious liberty and church-state separation. Americans for Religious Liberty is a national interfaith educational organization dedicated to defending religious freedom and separation of church and state.

We maintain that religious liberty is our most basic liberty, that this liberty can exist in full measure only when all levels and branches of government respect and adhere to the constitutional principle of separation of church and state, which requires at least that government operate with neutrality toward all religions and religious bodies, and that any deviation form that constitutionally mandated neutrality is one of those "experiments on our liberties" against which James Madison warned in his "Memorial and Remonstrance."

The Holy See is the headquarters of a church. That is the reason for its importance and the reason why more than 100 nations maintain diplomatic relations with it. The fact that the Holy See is primarily and essentially a religious entity is precisely why the United States government should not have diplomatic relations with it.

The president's action is not, as one senator has said, a resumption of the relations which our government had with the Papal States from 1797 to 1867. Those were consular and, later, ministerial relations of a purely secular nature with a very real state, which ceased to exist when it was incorporated into the Kingdom of Italy in 1870. The relationship which the president is setting up now is with the Holy See, a religious entity, and not with the sovereign microstate of Cittá del Vaticano. That this relationship is with a church is borne out by the fact that the Holy See concluded treaties with nations between 1870 and 1929 while its physical location, the Vatican, did not enjoy sovereignty.

While possible litigation to challenge U.S. diplomatic relations with the Holy See might present problems having nothing to do with the constitutionality of the relations, this does not release the executive and legislative branches from their sworn obligation to conform to the strictures imposed by the Constitution and Bill of Rights.

Establishment of diplomatic relations with the Holy See is objectionable on constitutional and public policy grounds because:

- It has the unconstitutional effect of preferring one religion over all others;
- It unconstitutionally creates the potential for excessive government entanglement between our government and a church;
- It creates new and exacerbates old tensions between faiths, as the public reactions to this appointment by individuals and religious bodies have made clear;
- It unconstitutionally creates the potential for political division along religious lines;

- It implies, in Madison's words, that "the Civil Magistrate . . . may employ Religion as an engine of Civil Policy . . . [which is] an unhallowed perversion of the means of salvation" ("Memorial and Remonstrance");
- It conveys to Americans not of the faith represented by the Holy See the impression that their government regards their faiths as second class;
- It blurs our uniquely American constitutional dividing line between church and state;
- It necessitates unconstitutional congressional appropriation or reprogramming of funds for the costs of maintaining an embassy to the Holy See;
- By violating the spirit and the letter of the First Amendment, it renders that guarantee of religious liberty more vulnerable to other forms of erosion and attack.

Although the Supreme Court has not had occasion to rule on the establishment of diplomatic relations with a church, its rulings in church-state cases cast grave doubt on the constitutionality of such actions. The thrust of the rulings is that the Establishment Clause is violated if a government action prefers one religion over another, lacks a clearly secular purpose, has a primary effect which advances or inhibits religion, fosters an excessive government entanglement with religion, or fosters political division along religious lines. While the president may claim a secular purpose for his action, the non-secular, preferential, and potentially entangling effects of diplomatic relations with the Holy See clearly run counter to the Court's tests of constitutionality.

It is said that diplomatic relations with the Holy See would promote peace and justice. But the Holy See's potential for contributions to peace and justice lie in its being a spiritual entity, and not in its possession of a 108-acre microstate. Further, it is distressing that this administration seems to be implying that a religious body would withhold information or aid that could advance peace or justice on account of its not being accorded diplomatic recognition.

Our nation has provided more religious liberty than any other because it has ever more fully implemented and adhered to the principle of separation of church and state. In this respect our country is unique and stands as a shining example to the rest of the world. The House, we believe, must uphold the First Amendment in spirit and letter, preserve church-state separation, promote interfaith harmony, and maintain the equality of all religious bodies and faiths before the law by refusing to appropriate or reprogram any funds to maintain any form of diplomatic relations with the Holy See or any other religious body.

The Catholic Church Routinely Ignores Child Sexual Abuse by Clergy*

On July 23, 2003, Massachusetts Attorney General Thomas E. Reilly released a groundbreaking and finely detailed report entitled "The Sexual Abuse of Children in the Roman Catholic Archdiocese of Boston." (The eighty-four page report is available in its entirety on the attorney general's website at www.ago.state.ma.us/archdiocese.pdf.)

In January 2002, Catholic priest John Geoghan was convicted of molesting a boy and sentenced to ten years in prison. More than 130 people had accused him of sexual abuse over a period of many years; other criminal charges, as well as several civil lawsuits, were pending against him. Geoghan's case is important because it led to the exposure of massive scandals regarding clerical sex abuse of minors.

Clerical sexual abuse of minors in Massachusetts is of public concern because it is a serious crime, as is the cover-up of such abuse by ecclesiastical authorities. And such sexual abuse isn't confined to Massachusetts or the United States, but it is a long-festering worldwide problem of staggering magnitude.

A Massive Cover-up

Sexual abuse of minors isn't confined to Catholic priests or even to clergy generally. Parents, relatives, teachers, scout leaders, various authority figures, and strangers are also guilty of these crimes. But nowhere has the abuse of minors been so protected or systematically covered up as in the nation's and the world's largest top-down-run religious organization. And rank-and-file Catholics are just as concerned about this problem as anyone else.

---

*This article, originally titled "A Culture of Clergy Sexual Abuse," was published in the book *Child Abuse* (Greenhaven Press, 2006). It appeared originally in the November-December 2003 issue of *The Humanist*.

In his introduction to the report, Reilly states:

Based on my conclusions and in order to ensure that children will be safe in the future, this report is essential; it is essential to create an official public record of what occurred. This mistreatment of children was so massive and so prolonged that it borders on the unbelievable. This report will confirm to all who may read it now and in the future, that this tragedy was real.

Reilly states that [Boston] archdiocese records show "that at least 789 victims (or third parties acting on the behalf of victims) have complained directly to the Archdiocese," that the "number of alleged victims who have disclosed their abuse likely exceeds one thousand. And the number increases even further when considering that an unknown number of victims likely have not, and may never disclose their abuses to others."

Reilly's report adds:

For more than fifty years there has been an institutional acceptance within the Archdiocese of clergy sexual abuse of children. Clergy sexual abuse of children has also been shown to be a nationwide problem with some reports indicating that more than 300 priests were removed from ministry in 2002 alone as a result of allegations of sexual abuse of children, and as many as 1,200 Roman Catholic priests in the United States have been accused of sexually abusing more than 4,000 children. The staggering magnitude of the problem would have alerted any reasonable, responsible manager that immediate and decisive measures must be taken.

Molesters are Protected

The report adds that the archdiocese's "investigation and discipline process . . . protects priests at the expense of victims and, in the final analysis, is incapable of leading to timely and appropriate responses to sex abuse allegations."

Reilly's report concludes:

The Archdiocese's responses to reports of sexual abuse of children, including maintaining secrecy of reports, placed children at risk. Top Archdiocese officials . . . decided that they should conceal—from the parishes, the laity, law enforcement and the public—their knowledge of individual complaints of abuse and the long history of such complaints within the Archdiocese. . . . The Archdiocese believed that Canon Law—the church's internal policies and procedures—prohibited it from reporting abuse to civil authorities in most instances . . . and the resulting publicity would harm the reputation of the Church. . . . In the very few case where allegations of sexual abuse of children were communicated to law enforcement, senior Archdiocese managers remained committed to the primary objectives—safeguarding the well-being of priests and the institution over the welfare of children and preventing scandal—and often failed to advise law enforcement authorities of all relevant information they possessed, including the full extent of the alleged abuser's history of abusing children.

An appendix to Reilly's report shows that between 1994 and 2000 the Boston archdiocese paid out $17,870,482 to settle legal claims from 402 victims, plus $1,157,219 for treatment costs to victims and $702,770 for treatment of priest abusers. Extrapolating from this data, it seems reasonable to agree with published estimates that since 1990 Catholic dioceses in the United States have paid out more than $1 billion to abuse victims—and that may only be the beginning.

In late August 2003 the Catholic Diocese of Covington, Kentucky, one of the church's smaller judicatories, released a report showing that since 1989 it had paid nearly $780,000 to abuse victims, $722,000 for counseling, and $218,000 in legal fees. The diocese also announced that it would begin talking with twenty-two people who have filed a $50 million suit charging clergy sex abuse. The Covington diocese also disclosed that 8 percent (30 of 372) of diocesan priests had sexually abused one or more minors over the past 50 years. . . .

Thousands Abused

Reilly's report confirms and is confirmed by the extraordinary and important book *Pederasty in the Catholic Church: Sexual Crimes of the Clergy Against Minors, a Drama Silenced and Covered Up by the Bishops . . .* by Spanish psychologist Pepe Rodriguez. Rodriguez covers pretty much the same ground as Reilly, but in greater depth and scope, replete with case histories, covering not only the United States but also Spain, Latin America, and elsewhere.

Rodriguez' book, up to date as of September 2002, makes clear that the problem of sexual abuse of minors by religious authority figures is aggravated by two factors: the understandable reluctance of victims to report abuse and the longstanding but largely unwritten policy of church officials, from the pope on down, to coddle abusers and go to great lengths to cover up abuse. Both Rodriguez . . . and Reilly . . . detail the church policy of transferring abusers from one parish to another, one diocese to another, and even one country to another.

Rodriguez notes that various estimates of the number of priests, and even bishops, who abuse minors range from 3 percent to 6 percent, though the figure for Spain may be even higher, with the Covington, Kentucky, diocese weighing in at 8 percent. The number of victims worldwide will never be known but certainly goes well into the many tens of thousands.

Most Priests Are Sexually Active

Rodriguez' 2002 book builds on his 1995 book, *The Sex Life of the Clergy*. In this remarkably thorough earlier book, the Spanish psychologist covers even broader ground. His studies in traditionally Catholic Spain show that 60 percent of priests are sexually active in violation of their celibacy vows. Of these, his study found, 53 percent had relations with adult females, 21 percent with adult males, 14 percent with minor males, and 12 percent with minor females. He notes that a large number of Spanish priests left the priesthood to marry and that others formed long-term relationships ignored by both the laity and the church hierarchy. . . .

Rodriguez recommends that instances of sexual abuse be reported to police or civil authorities, as complaining to church authorities is likely to lead nowhere, though hopefully the expanding scandal . . . might possibly improve the situation.

Earth, Air, Water, Fire

The ancients were right
Our world is composed of four elements
Earth, air, water, and fire

Earth is –
Iowa topsoil washing down the Mississippi to the gulf
Parched barrens in Amazonia where lush forests once stood
scarred stripmined hills in West Virginia
what is hidden under spreading asphalt and shopping malls
overgrazed deserts-in-formation in Africa
thin layers, laced with toxic chemicals

Air is –
Invisible – except for its contaminants
where we dump our chloroflurocarbons and nitrous oxides and carbon
    dioxide and a thousand other chemicals
what carries away soil from worn out fields
moving untapped over shores and plains

Water is –
what we need
what all plants and animals need
at the bottom of emptying aquifers
the receptacle of our untreated wastes
what we pour into marginal soils in California

Fire is –
the oxidation of carbohydrates in the cells of five billion humans
the explosion of petrochemicals in millions of inefficient internal combustion
    engines and power generators
the burning of trees in Amazonia and Madagascar
the second Law of Thermodynamics responding to human thoughtlessness
the sun's daily flood of energy going unused
what propels bullets, shells, rockets, tanks, bombers, and warships as men
    strive for control of our shrinking earth, air, and water
what we need in our brains and bellies if our children are to enjoy their fair
    share of our earth, air and water

From *Images*, 1991.

The Righteous Ones

They came from far and wide
They arrived in their BMWs and Jaguars
Their Cadillacs and Lincoln Town Cars
Important men
Tall tanned men with trophy girlfriends
Pale pudgy men with briefcases
Grey-haired men in three-piece suits
They came to hear their leader
One just like themselves only more so
The leader raised his arms and spoke:

Oh Lord, shower thy blessings on those here gathered

> (Response)
> *For we are the righteous ones*

Bless those who by their accomplishments merit thy bounty

> *For we are the righteous ones*

Bless those who are servants of thy mighty purposes

> *For we are the righteous ones*

We thank thee for bestowing upon us the benefits earned by our diligence and skill and cleverness

> *For we are the righteous ones*

Hear, oh Lord, our prayer that our efforts to produce on this earth a paradise to reward thy disciples will reflect thy magnificent glory

> *For we are the righteous ones*

Now, oh Lord, we join our voices together in thy Holy Name to concentrate our thoughts on the tasks at hand

On those less righteous and worthy than we

> *Let us prey*

On the weak and unlucky

> *Let us prey*

On the ignorant and the gullible

> *Let us prey*

On the poor and the dependent

> *Let us prey*

On the drones with their unions and their grievances

Let us prey

On the elderly who have outlived their usefulness

Let us prey

On the malcontents and critics

Let us prey

On the bounties of nature thou hast given us for our wise use

Let us prey

On those whose looks and accents differ appreciably from our own

Let us prey

On all who question the Rules

Let us prey

On all who question the System

Let us heap scorn

On all who dispute Duly Constituted Authority

Let us heap scorn

On all who challenge the Right Order of things

Let us heap scorn

On all who bandy catchphrases like Social Justice

Let us heap scorn

On all who fail to appreciate our worthiness

Let us heap scorn

Hear and bless us, oh Lord

The important men
The tall tanned men with trophy girlfriends
The pale pudgy men with briefcases
The grey-haired men in three piece suits
Paused for a moment of silent prayer and meditation
Then they got back into their BMWs and Jaguars
Their Cadillacs and Lincoln Town Cars
And went about their business
For they are the righteous ones.

From *Six Stories and Seventy Poems*, 2001.

Letters to the Editor

S.D. voters reject another theocratic initiative

Washington Examiner, November 13, 2006

South Dakota voters' 55-45 rejection of a draconian anti-abortion ballot issue on Nov. 7 is a great victory for common sense, religious freedom and women's rights. Had this harsh measure passed, women would have lost their right to freedom of conscience and a sectarian theology would have been imposed on all women--both in serious violation of the First Amendment.

Let's also remember that in 2004, South Dakota voters also wisely defeated a measure that would have allowed the state to compel taxpayers to help support discriminatory faith-based private schools.

☜

Nearly half of world's population lives in misery

Washington Examiner, October 24, 2006

Re: "Overpopulation worries forget ultimate resource," Oct. 19

It's easy for Jonah Goldberg to scoff at statements by Lawrence, Shaw, Wells, and others long gone, but he and the late Julian Simon are wrong about our not having a serious population/environment problem.

Our oceans are overfished, deforestation and desertification are rapidly shrinking the amont of useful land, soils are being exhausted, oil will eventually run out, many millions are without potable water, nearly half of the world's six billion people live in misery without adequate food, medical care, or education. The US, Europe, Japan, and Australia are not doing badly because we can exploit the resources of the globe. Our populations are stable, but overpopulation is devastating the developing world. Add to that the very real problem of global warming.

Sticking one's head in the sand is no answer.

Santorum's Catholic comments embarrass

Wilkes Barre (PA) *Times Leader*, October 22, 2006

Senator Rick Santorum is an embarrassment. Addressing an Opus Dei gathering in Rome in January 2002 (per National Catholic Reporter correspondent John Allen) Santorum declared, "I regard George W. Bush as the first Roman Catholic president [of the United States]". What about John F. Kennedy? Well, Santorum has disparaged Kennedy's strong support for religious freedom and church-state separation during his 1960 presidential campaign. Surely Pennsylvania can do better.

And Speaking of Islamo-Fascism . . .

The Nation, October 16, 2006

Re Katha Pollit's September 25 mention of "noted foreign policy expert" Rick Santorum, Ricky, addressing an Opus Dei gathering in Rome in January 2002 (per National Catholic Reporter correspondent John Allen), declared, "I regard George W. Bush as the first Roman Catholic president of the United States". What about JFK? Well, Ricky thinks that JFK was all wet in his fall 1960 defense of church-state separation. Say goodbye, Rick.

School voucher supporters ignore public polls

Washington Examiner, October 13, 2006

The Milton Friedman Foundation's study on school vouchers was way off target. School vouchers would fragment our school populations along sectarian, class, ethnic and other lines while raising educational costs.

The August 2006 Gallup poll showed that public opposition to vouchers is 60 percent to 36 percent, which is close to the 2-to-1 opposition to vouchers registered in 25 statewide referendums in recent years. D.C. voters rejected a voucher-like plan in 1981 by 89 percent to 11 percent.

Gallup found that respondents rated inadequate financing as the biggest problem facing public schools. Three-fourths of parents have a dim view of President Bush's "No Child Left Behind" law and 81 percent believe the gap between white and minority students can be narrowed without sacrificing standards.

Finally, school vouchers violate three-fourths of state constitutions, including ours.

'Personhood begins much later than conception'

Washington Examiner, October 10, 2006

Doug Bandow ("Liberalism unbound ..., Oct 6) is 180 degrees off target in his piece on abortion rights. He ducks the basic question: Who should make decisions about ending pregnancies, the individual women or politicians?

He also makes the mistake of equating fetuses with people. In the Judeo-Christian tradition personhood does not begin until months after conception. Neuroscience proves that the functions of personhood are not possible until some time after 28-32 weeks, when the cerebral cortex is sufficiently developed to permit consciousness.

The Supreme Court was right in 1973 in *Roe v Wade*.

Apologize to Iran

National Catholic Reporter, October 6, 2006

Your editorial on the United States and Iran was right on target (*NCR*, Sept. 22). Too few pundits are even mentioning that our troubles with Iran began with our inexcusable overthrow of the Mossadegh government in 1953. It's probably too late to put the toothpaste back in the tube, but we might start with an apology to the people of Iran.

A Delay in Family Planning

Washington Post, October 2, 2006

Sarah Epstein is right that family planning is essential to combating world hunger and poverty (letter, Sept 22).

A report ordered decades ago by President Richard M. Nixon concluded that universal availability of family planning information and wherewithal is necessary to prevent a host of evils and to protect US interests. Unfortunately, the report was classified and buried until almost the eve of the 1994 Cairo population conference, at which President Bill Clinton offered similar proposals.

It's a crying shame that the Reagan, Bush I, and Bush II administrations have seen fit to ignore these problems.

ᗒᗕ

Prayer in schools

Washington Times, September 20, 2006

A Baylor University poll ("Belief in God ..., Sept 12) finds that 70% of respondents "would allow prayer in schools". Too many Americans assume that students can't pray in school. That is totally wrong. Every student has the right to pray in school. The Supreme Court outlawed only government sponsored or government mandated prayer.

Every student may pray whenever and however he or she pleases or has been taught at home or church. There is no such thing as a one size fits all prayer.

ᗒᗕ

Don't compare Islamic terrorists to Nazis

Washington Examiner, September 20, 2006

Tim Dudenhoefer's comparison of today's Islamic terrorists with yesterday's Nazis (letter, Sept 18) is absurd — like comparing cabbages to mangoes.

The Nazi regime was a tightly controlled totalitarian nation. The Nazis' surrender in May 1945 ended World War II [in Europe].

Today's Islamic terrorists are no nation, have no boundaries and are a loose movement scattered from the UK to Indonesia. Anyone following the news since our mistaken invasion of Iraq knows that there are more terrorists now than four years ago.

Past administrations set up present conflict with Iran

Washington Examiner, September 13, 2006

Our problems with Iran did not begin with Jimmy Carter but, rather, with the US overthrow of Iran's elected government in 1953. The spread of terrorism in the last four years is due to the Bush administration's failure to capture Osama bin Laden in Afghanistan and its stupid, unnecessary invasion of Iraq in 2003.

Plus the Reagan administration's helping both sides [in the Iran-Iraq war] in the 1980s and its support for the most reactionary element, the Taliban, in the Afghan struggle against the USSR.

Iranians have good reason to dislike US

Washington Examiner, September 5, 2006

Much has been written about Iran's support for terrorists — Hezbollah, the Taliban, etc., but little about why Iran dislikes the US so much.

In 1953 the Eisenhower administration did what the Truman administration had refused to do: It overthrew the legitimate government of Iranian Prime Minister Mohammad Mossadegh and installed as dictator Shah Reza Pahlavi, whose repressive government and secret police led to the "Islamic revolution" of Ayatollah Khomeini in 1979 and Iran's turn to fundamentalist fanaticism. The details are laid out in Stephen Kinzer's book "All the Shah's Men".

By the way, the US overthrow of Iran's government was promoted by UK Prime Minister Winston Churchill to protect British colonialist oil operations there, the company now known as BP.

Of course Iran's present government is a troublemaking tyranny, thanks to a major US blunder over fifty years ago.

President Bush's costly misadventure in Iraq will probably cause even more trouble.

☙

Productivity and the paycheck

New York Times, September 3, 2006

With wages falling and corporate profits rising since George W. Bush took office, it is time for wage earners - most Americans - to install a Congress in November more sensitive to the needs of ordinary people, including the increasing numbers of the poor.

☙

Voting against school choice

Washington Times, August 26, 2006

The editorial, "A question of bias" (Tuesday), criticized the 2006 Phi Delta Kappa/Gallup poll, which found that respondents opposed school vouchers 60% to 36% and that by 71% to 24% they preferred improving public schools over "finding an alternative system. The editorial then asserted that "school choice and voucher programs are popular with the public".

The truth, however, is that the PDK/Gallup findings are supported by the best sort of opinion poll, a statewide referendum vote. In 25 such referenda from coast to coast voters have rejected vouchers or their analogs by an average percentage of two to one.

The PDK/Gallup poll also found that 88% of respondents rated their children's public schools satisfactory to excellent.

☙

Lieberman should retire

Washington Examiner, August 14, 2006

Senator Lieberman, having been rejected by his own party's voters, should now just retire gracefully. His campaigning as an independent can only harm his reputation, his party, his state, and his country.

C'mon, Joe, it's time to go.

Being free to be

Washington Examiner, August 8, 2006

Suzanne Fields' column "Storm in a small town" (Op-Ed, Thursday) was right on the mark. She wisely noted that our country's founders "bequeathed [to us] a government that separates church and state, protecting each of us in his or her faith". The narrow sectarians in the small town in Delaware appear to have much the same mentality as the Islamists in the Middle East.

Religion has thrived in America precisely because the wise men who wrote the Constitution and Bill of Rights had learned from colonial and European history that separation of church and state is best for religion, best for democratic government, and best for religious freedom.

Examiner should talk to some scientists

Washington Examiner, July 26, 2006

RE: "Defending Intelligent Design after Dover"

Patrick Gavin's interview with the authors of "Traipsing Into Evolution" (July 19) was quite one-sided. In addition, none of the authors of the book is actually a scientist.

May I suggest that the Examiner interview a real scientist on this subject, such as anthropologist Dr Eugenie Scott, head of the National Center for Science Education and author the 2004 book "Evolution vs. Creationism: An Introduction".

Separating church and state

Washington Times, July 6, 2006

In his column "Explosive facts" (Commentary, Tuesday), Thomas Sowell notes that the phrase "separation of church and state" does not appear in the constitution. OK, but the principle is implied because the Constitution does not give government any power to meddle with religion.

In 1802, President Jefferson, with the concurrence of Attorney General Levi Lincoln, wrote that the First amendment erects "a wall of separation between church and state." As early as 1879, the Supreme Court agreed with Jefferson, as did Supreme Courts from 1947 on. Further, nearly all state constitutions contain church-state separation provisions. And in 1952, Congress approved the Puerto Rican Constitution, which declares, "There shall be complete separation of church and state." In 1959, Congress approved constitutions for the new states of Alaska and Hawaii, both of which include the separation principle and specifically bar the use of public funds to aid faith-based schools.

America is supposed to be about freedom and liberty, not government restrictions on our basic, hard-won liberties.

'Bushisms'

The Progressive, July 2006

In Will Durst's haste to compile a list of descriptives [a whole page of them!] for the Bush Administration ("Impeachment? No. Impalement!" June issue), he overlooked a few: sleazy, goofy, dimwitted, crackbrained, dopey, dull, pietistic, shifty-eyed, phony, harebrained, ecophobic, billionaire-brownnosing, grammarphobic, moronic, idiotic, indifferent, Cheneyized, Rovist, incurious, antihumanistic, Potemkinite, momzer, anal retentive, Kafkaesque, Orwellian, loco, nutty, small-minded, cerebrally disadvantaged, nausea-inducing, disgusting, paparazzi-courting, pusillanimous, war-loving. In my haste, I have probably overlooked others.

Founding Religion

First Things, June/July 2006

Michael Novak's "The Truth About Religious Freedom" (March) was somewhat out of focus. The Founders endorsed the Declaration of Independence's assertion that our rights are granted by the Creator, but how does one explain why this was discovered only in 1776? Since we were a weak, divided nation fighting the most powerful empire in the world, doesn't it seem likely that Jefferson asserted the "divine rights of the people" as a public relations attack on the "divine right of kings"? Whatever the Creator had in mind, in the real world we acquired rights by defining them, asserting them, fighting for them, and building the machinery to defend them.

Novak writes that the First Amendment was designed to "prevent any one religion" from being established. But by 1787 single-church establishments had either disappeared or given was to "multiple establishments". As the Supreme Court noted in 1879 in the Reynolds decision, Jefferson was right when he wrote, with the concurrence of Attorney General Lincoln, that the First Amendment erected a wall of separation between church and state. Of course it took years to work out the bugs, but the Supreme Court was correct about separation in 1947 in Everson and later rulings.

Novak insults those whose ethics are based on naturalism rather than supernaturalism. Are religious injunctions against murder, theft, and bearing false witness valid because the Creator said so, or did religions credit the Creator with injunctions that people worked out from their experience of living in society?

☞

'Film protest'

National Catholic Reporter, June 30, 2006

Tom Roberts' comments about "The Last Temptation of Christ" in his editor's note (NCR, May 26) remind me of when I went to see the premiere of the Nikos Kazantzakis film in Washington. There were more demonstrators parading outside the theater than there were people inside. The demonstrators carried all manner of protest signs and even a life-size statue of Christ.

Ironically, the marchers repeatedly passed a homeless drunk lying unconscious in the gutter in front of the theater scarcely three feet from them. Not one so much as noticed him. It occurred to me that the marchers were more concerned about shadows on a screen than what Jesus would have said and done had he been there.

'Another Inconvenient Truth'

Science Times, June 27, 2006

"Next Victim of Warming: The Beaches" (June 20) corroborates Al Gore's thesis in his film and book "An Inconvenient Truth". When will enough people and politicians wake up?

Reproductive Choice

Chicago Tribune (online), June 14, 2006

Regarding Judy Peres' "States set stage for bans on abortion" (June 12), if opponents of reproductive choice succeed in getting each state to set its own abortion policies, then every woman's basic right to decide whether and when to have a child will change every time she crosses a state line.

Anti-choicer Clarke Forsythe says the right to decide should be "returned to the people". But that's exactly what Roe v. Wade did. Roe did return the right to choose to the people, to the individual women who have problem pregnancies.

The drive to deny women reproductive freedom of choice is based on bad theology, bad history, bad science, and the half-concealed desire to perpetuate male dominance over women.

U.S. defeated the Nazis in less time

Washington Examiner, June 13, 2006

My son served as a US Navy officer on a warship in harm's way in the

Persian Gulf during the 1980s Iran-Iraq war. So I feel justified in criticizing President George W. Bush and Vice President Dick Cheney – the two guys in the White House, who, having avoided combat themselves, have nonetheless felt free to send young Americans to Iraq to kill and be killed, to wound and be wounded, and all for a lie.

The US and the world are less secure now than before their Mesopotamian misadventure, which incidentally has lasted longer than our ground combat against the Nazis in World War II.

Sectarian subsidies offend Constitution

Baltimore Sun, June 2, 2006

The decisions by Gov. Robert L. Ehrlich Jr. [Republican] and Mayor Martin O'Malley [Democrat] to provide grants totaling $447,500 for a National Baptist Convention event to be held this month in Baltimore is not only a violation of the First Amendment but also a shameless effort to troll for votes ("Support of religious conference criticized", May 27).

Not only that, but the convention will reportedly contain sessions that can only be regarded as tax-subsidized attacks on the religions of other Maryland-ers.

Politicians of both parties should avoid pandering for sectarian votes.

The practice threatens the religious liberty of all of us, smells too much like the kind of politico-religious extremism that we supposedly oppose in the Middle East, and can only further reduce respect for politicians and the political process.

(Untitled)

Laurel (MD) *Leader*, June 1, 2006

Mathew Pasalic's May 18 letter on church-state separation is just plain wrong.

While the phrase "separation of church and state" does not appear in the

Constitution, it is implied, as the Constitution gives government no authority to meddle with religion. The First amendment prohibits government from interfering with the free exercise of religion or taking any action "respecting an establishment of religion." President Jefferson declared in 1802 that these words erect "a wall of separation between church and state." The Supreme Court in the 1870s agreed with Jefferson, as did the Court, unanimously, in 1947 in the *Everson* and subsequent rulings.

After the Civil War the Fourteenth Amendment was passed to make the Bill of Rights applicable to state and local governments. In 1952 Congress approved the Puerto Rico constitution, which states: "There shall be complete separation of church and state."

The late Chief Justice Rehnquist may have disagreed with the separation principle, but he was outvoted by his colleagues.

As for religion classes in public schools, there is no way that our many hundreds of religious traditions and divisions within them could possibly provide such classes in our 15,000 separate school districts. Our churches are quite capable of taking care of religious education.

Moreover, Benjamin Franklin wrote 250 years ago that, "When a religion is good, I conceive it will support itself; and when it does not support itself, and God does not take care to support it so that its professors [adherents] are obliged to call for the help of the civil power [government], 'tis a sign, I apprehend, of its being a bad one."

Government's inaction on rate, gas hikes frustrates

Montgomery Gazette, May 24, 2006

Pepco has just informed customers that residential electric rates will go up in June by 41 percent, an average of $66 monthly, $792 annually. We are paying more than $3 per gallon for gasoline, with no relief in sight. And we have yet to feel the tremendous ripple effect of these increases on the prices of everything we have to buy.

Yet the federal and state governments have done nothing significant.

As individuals and families we can effect economies, but not near enough to make any real difference. Government must step in. We need an immediate and serious effort to harness power from wind and to use hydrogen. We need to greatly increase vehicle gas mileage through tax incentives.

Employers could help by using a four-day work week or a nine-day work fortnight.

More delay will only hurt the vast majority of us whose incomes have been static for 25 years.

Budget reform proposal burdens future generations

Washington Examiner, May 12, 2006

Brian Riedl's proposals for budget reform can only widen the existing canyon between the super-rich and the rest of us.

Fiscal sanity requires that Congress leave the estate tax in place, roll back Bush's tax cuts that favor the wealthy, modestly raise the cap on Social Security payroll payments and cut the pork and special breaks for the rich.

Rising oil costs will ripple through the economy and further hurt the tens of millions of families whose incomes have remained stalled for 20 years.

Bill Clinton left office with a surplus. George W. Bush will leave office with a huge fiscal millstone hanging around the necks of our grandchildren.

Grant for religious conference goes against church-state separation

Maryland Gazette, April 12, 2006

Gov. Robert Ehrlich's inclusion in his supplemental budget of $150,000 for a sectarian religious conference in June shows contempt for the First Amendment, the constitutional provision that is supposed to protect the religious freedom of every American.

This grant would violate every Marylander's right to voluntarily support only the religious institutions of their free choice.

Benjamin Franklin wrote 250 years ago that there is something wrong when a religion calls on the government for financial help. Curiously, this grant would go for a Baptist affair, yet Baptists from Roger Williams on helped pioneer religious freedom and church-state separation.

What is even worse is that Gov. Ehrlich appears to be using this grant to buy votes in November.

James Madison, architect of the Bill of Rights, wrote in 1785 that a politician who employs "religion as an engine of civil policy" makes "an unhallowed perversion of the means of salvation."

The General Assembly should reject this egregious attack on religious freedom.

∽❧

'Poor running mate"

Washington Times, April 4, 2006

The Washington Times reported on the defeat in the Maryland House of Delegates of effort to extend the statute of limitations for dealing with sexual abuse of minors, apparently at the behest of some church leaders ("Delegate's shift baffles victims of church abuse," Metropolitan, Friday). The same day, *The Times* reported on the still rising payouts by Catholic Church officials for clerical sexual abuse and its elaborate coverup. To date, this has cost church officials in the U.S. $1.3 billion ("Catholic sex-abuse payouts still rising," Page 1, Friday).

Of course, this problem is not confined to the U.S. It is an equally serious problem in Canada, Ireland, Spain and many other countries as well. It also has seriously hurt the reputation of the Catholic Church.

Delegate Anthony Brown's cave-in on this issue makes him a poor running mate for gubernatorial aspirant Martin O'Malley.

∽❧

History may not treat Bush kindly

Washington Examiner, April 3, 2006

Malcolm Lawrence writes that President George W. Bush "will emerge as one of the best presidents in the history of our nation." Surely he jests.

Bush lied us into an unnecessary war that has killed more than 2,300 and wounded more than 17,000 young Americans, badly tarnished our image around the world, made the U.S. and the world less secure, fueled Islamic extremism and plunged our grandchildren deep into debt.

He has shown incompetence in dealing with the hurricane damage, polarized our population, undermined the Bill of Rights, made the poor poorer and the rich richer, weakened American education, increased unnecessary secrecy in government, concentrated too much power in the executive branch and stimulated the politicization of religion.

Great? No way!

∽✦

The Year of Two Popes

The Atlantic Monthly, April 2006

Paul Elie's "Year of Two Popes" (January/February *Atlantic*) was an interesting tour of the rarefied atmosphere of the inner workings of the Holy See, but it scarcely touched on the real situation of the Catholic Church here on Planet Earth.

The Church in Ireland is in free fall in the wake of the Ferns Report on clergy sexual abuse. In Spain, psychologist Pepe Rodriguez has published two major studies on the same problem. In the United States, the clergy abuse scandals have not abated and could end up costing the Church billions, while donations, church attendance, and parochial-school enrollments have plummeted over the past third of a century.

If the Holy See could come down to earth, get over its obsessions with contraception, abortion rights, in vitro fertilization, divorce, homosexuality, and male dominance – obsessions that most First World Catholics do not share – and concentrate on the social-justice and ethical teachings of the Nazarene carpenter, it could make enormous contributions toward helping to solve the myriad real problems facing humankind today.

∽✦

Victims are owed right to sue abusers

Baltimore Sun, March 28, 2006

Efforts by Maryland's top Catholic Church officials to defeat bills in Annapolis that would extend the time for victims of childhood sexual abuse to file lawsuits against abusers and their employers, including clergy and church officials, should be seen as just another attempt to cover up the worldwide clergy pedophile scandal.

What do these officials have to fear?

Exposure of their negligence in dealing with the problem? Having to compensate the victims of abuse for the damage to their lives and mental health?

There should be no limits on the pursuit of civil or criminal remedies for child abuse, especially by members of the clergy or other trusted adults.

Religion, state should be separate

Keene (New Hampshire) *Sentinel*, March 23, 2006

Eric Moskowitz's March 10 piece on the defeat of vouchers in the House notes that voucher proponents said their plan was constitutional because the public funds could only be spent "on the nonreligious portion of education at religious schools."

That is an illusion. In theory and practice the whole curriculum in faith-based schools is permeated with a particular religious point of view.

The New Hampshire constitution clearly provides that "no money raised by taxation shall ever be granted or applied for the use of the schools or institutions of any religious sect or denomination."

The drama of 'Crash'

Washington Times, March 15, 2006

William Tucker accuses the Oscar-winning film "Crash" (Culture, et cetera, yesterday) of pushing the "Hollywood" idea that "everyone is a racist." He must have seen a different film than the one I saw.

"Crash," though not a box-office smash, deserved the Academy Award for best picture for dramatically demonstrating that humans are very complicated; that life is in shades of gray rather than "Hollywood" black and white in Technicolor; that people have mixed motives and experiences; that we should not rush to judgment; and, quite simply, that "Crash," like "Lone Star," "Mother Night," "Death and the Maiden" and other great films, provides both first-rate drama and a useful set of moral lessons. Like Shakespeare's plays.

Matt Dillon's cop is far more interesting and complex than unidimensional "stars" like Arnold Schwarzenegger.

❧

School vouchers and teachers

Washington Times, March 6, 2006

Thomas Sowell's "Something for nothing: Part II" (Commentary, Friday) attacked teacher unions for opposing school vouchers in order to protect their jobs. But without their democratic unions teachers would be little better off than street sweepers (not that there is anything wrong with street sweepers). Few people would go to the trouble and expense of becoming teachers if they didn't have some job protection from the sometimes arbitrary decisions of cheapskate school boards.

Private, mostly faith-based, school teachers earn less than public school teachers, rarely have job protection, enjoy selected student bodies and are generally selected on the basis of their religion.

It should be added that University of Illinois researchers Christopher and Sarah Lubienski reported this year that a large statistical analysis of school math scores shows that on average public school students score higher than private or charter schools students. Another study released this year shows that student performance is directly related to family income and level of parents' education.

Finally, 25 statewide referendums from coast to coast over the last 40 years, plus numerous opinion polls, show that the American public is strongly opposed to school vouchers.

❧

Tax support undermines religious freedom

Maryland Gazette, March 3, 2006

Lt. Gov. Michael S. Steele's trolling for votes by promoting tax support for faith-based charities is wrong.

It undermines the right of all citizens not to be forced by government to support religious enterprises, in violation of our time-honored principle of church-state separation.

Ben Franklin wisely observed 250 years ago that there is something seriously wrong with a religion when it cannot support itself.

Why can't people of many faiths or none join together to support nonsectarian soup kitchens, homeless shelters, clinics for the poor, etc.? Are some people afraid to work with people of other religions?

A proliferation of tax-supported faith-based charities can only fragment efforts to help the needy, promote unregulated operations of often questionable efficacy, and undermine public charities.

Steele, like President Bush, seems not to care about one of the core values of our democracy, religious freedom.

☙

Teaching the Faith

First Things, March, 2006

Father Neuhaus makes light of the controversy in the Golden State over the University of California's refusal to accept certain evangelical high schools' courses as meeting requirements for admission (While We're At It, January).

Two points to consider: The university is not telling the faith-based school what it must not teach, but, rather, what sorts of courses are necessary for admission to this particular university; and Neuhaus might well side with the university if he saw the anti-Catholicism that pervades many of the texts and courses in many conservative evangelical schools. This anti-Catholicism is well documented in Frances Paterson's book *Democracy and Intolerance* and Albert Menendez' book *Visions of Reality: What Fundamentalist Schools Teach.*

Menendez cites, for example, textbooks used in fundamentalist schools that call Catholicism "a perversion of biblical Christianity"; that say the papacy rests "upon a number of false assumptions"; that refer to "Romanist error," "pagan Catholicism"; that declare "The Southern states . . . saw themselves threatened by those holding . . . unbiblical beliefs, who were most numerous in the Northeast"; that hold the Mass is "unbiblical and idolatrous" and monasticism "has no justification in Scripture but derives from pagan influences on apostate Christianity"; that insists the Reformation was "a divine instrument for propagating religious truth in Catholic Europe"; and Jesuits are "a hellish conclave"; etc. Should such teaching prepare students for admission to a public university?

☙

Suspicion surrounds Catholic group

Washington Examiner, February 21, 2006

It's good that *Da Vinci Code* publisher Doubleday is bringing out an edition of Opus Dei founder Josemaria Escriva's little book, *The Way*. Having read it in the original Spanish, I can say that most readers will find it bizarre and hilariously medieval.

There is a vast literature about Opus Dei, most of it quite critical, by former members and other researchers.

Convicted spy and former FBI agent Robert Hanssen was an Opus Dei member. Since Hanssen told an Opus Dei priest, Robert Bucciarelli, about his spying for the Soviets, why didn't the priest notify the proper authorities? And what did Opus Dei do with the information?

Regarding religious freedom

Washington Times, February 21, 2006

Regarding the review of Kevin Hasson's "The Right to be Wrong" ("Maintaining religious freedom," Books, Sunday), Mr. Hasson is wrong if he thinks that the 14th Amendment did not apply the First Amendment to state and local government until the 1920s. The Congress that approved the 14th Amendment after the Civil War intended precisely that, though it took the Supreme Court 50 years to actually do it.

If Mr. Hasson believes that First Amendment free exercise is adequately protected, he should reread Justice Antonin Scalia's 1990 ruling in *Oregon v. Smith* to see how free exercise has been diluted.

If he thinks that free exercise eliminates the need for the establishment clause, he is mistaken, as the history of religious freedom in the United States makes clear.

Privatized education would divide nation

Washington Examiner, February 13, 2006

Dino Drudi's attack on public education was totally divorced from reality. Americans decided more than 150 years ago that education is a public responsibility. Annual Gallup polls show that the vast majority of parents are satisfied with public schools.

University of Illinois researchers published a study in January of 340,000 students in 13,000 public, private and charter schools, based on the 2003 National Assessment of Educational Progress, and found that public schools scored higher than both private (mostly faith-based) and charter schools.

Turning education over to the private sector would raise educational costs, make teaching a less desirable profession, and fragment our school population along religious, class, ethnic and other lines.

Many inner-city schools have problems because of residential segregation and inadequate and inequitably distributed tax support.

⌦

Renewable energy the way to independence

Washington Examiner, February 6, 2006

Carl Henn rightly criticizes President Bush's weak proposals for dealing with our oil addiction. Inexhaustible wind and solar energy are the answer, not more coal or nuclear power. And exploiting wind and solar energy would create a great many more domestic jobs.

President Bush also failed to push hard for energy conservation. We need far more efficient cars and taxes on gas-guzzlers, not to mention more energy-conserving appliances, houses and buildings.

As Henn points out, we must deal with runaway population growth, but President Bush has done all he can to impede efforts to solve the world overpopulation problem, even blocking congressional appropriations for the UN Population Fund, and reducing access to reproductive care services both in the U.S. and abroad.

We've known about these problems for 50 years, but have done far too little to address them. It's time to wake up and smell the coffee.

⌦

Committee hearings still are useful for choosing justices

Washington Examiner, January 30, 2006

Senate Judiciary Committee hearings on judicial nominees should not be scrapped, as they are the best way for the Senate and the public to find out exactly who will be interpreting the Constitution for many years to come.

Remember, such hearings spared the country the embarrassment and danger of having Robert Bork on the Supreme Court and came very close to blocking Clarence Thomas.

☞

A 'Reprehensible' Side of Federal Hurricane Aid

Education Week, January 25, 2006

Congress' high-handed provision of millions of dollars for vouchers for faith-based schools in Louisiana and Mississippi in the wake of Hurricane Katrina is a slap at both of those states' constitutions ("Congress Passes Hurricane Aid for Schools," Jan.4, 2006). The constitutions of both Louisiana (Article IV, Section 8; Article XII, Section 13) and Mississippi (Article VIII, Section 208) prohibit such aid.

It is simply wrong for any level of government to tax citizens for the support of faith-based schools that commonly practice forms of discrimination and indoctrination that would be intolerable in public schools. Using the Katrina catastrophe to chip away at public education is reprehensible.

Of course the young victims of Katrina need all the help Congress can provide, but it should be exclusively through the (already underfunded) public schools of their home communities, or wherever in the country these kids now attend school.

☞

Alito will tilt Supreme Court to the right

Washington Examiner, January 18, 2006

As the Supreme Court is presently constituted, Alito would very likely tilt the court away form women's rights, civil liberties and the constitutional principle of church-state separation that protects the religious liberty of all of us.

❧

President Carter's values

National Catholic Reporter, January 13, 2006

Thanks to Fr. Robert Drinan for his perceptive review of former President Jimmy Carter's new book Our Endangered Values (NCR, Dec. 16). Carter is a man whose Christian faith is far more deep, real and meaningful than that of the so-and-so currently in the White House.

Carter's definition of fundamentalism, which he also presented in an address to a Baptist conference in the United Kingdom in July 2005, is one of the best and most succinct I have seen.

We need more Baptists like Jimmy Carter and Bill Moyers and fewer of the Jerry Falwell or Pat Robertson type.

❧

Congress Using Katrina as Cover
to Promote Vouchers

Austin Chronicle (online), January 11, 2006

Congress' provision of millions of dollars for vouchers for faith-based schools in Louisiana, Mississippi, and possibly Texas in the wake of Hurricane Katrina is a slap at the constitutions of all three states, which prohibit such aid.

In 2004 the Baton Rouge *Advocate* found Louisianians opposed to vouchers 60% to 34%, and right after the Jan. 5 Florida Supreme court ruling against vouchers in that state, the AOL poll registered opposition to vouchers nationwide at 57% to 37%. These figures are similar to the two-to-one average opposition to vouchers or their analogues in 25 statewide referendum elections from coast to coast from 1967 to 2004.

It is wrong for government to tax citizens for the support of sectarian schools that commonly practice forms of discrimination and indoctrination that would be intolerable in public schools. Using Katrina to chip away at public education is reprehensible.

Of course the young Katrina victims need all the help Congress can provide, but it should be only through the public schools of their home communities or wherever in the country the kids now attend school.

෴

Support for Separation

Crisis, January 2006

Regarding John Rossomando's article "Back to the Roots: The Founders sand the Separation of Church and State" (October 2005), there is no one position of Catholics on church-state separation, a principle that is supported by a wide range of Catholics and other religious people, including the rather thin ranks of secularists.

Cardinal James Gibbons stated that "American Catholics rejoice in our separation of Church and State. . . . [I]t gives us liberty and binds together priests and people in a union better than Church and State." The late Cardinal Richard Cushing of Boston declared that "I don't know of anywhere in the history of Christianity where the Catholic Church, the Protestant Church, or any other church has made greater progress than in the United States of America; and in my opinion the chief reason is that there is no union of church and state"; and that "Catholics do not need the support of civil law to be faithful to their religious convictions, and they do not seek to impose by law their moral views on other members of society."

John F. Kennedy said, "I believe in an America where the separation of church and state is absolute . . . where no church or church school is granted any public funds or political preference." Rev. Robert Drinan was a staunch supporter of church-state separation during his five terms in Congress and said in the Boston *Herald-Traveler*, regarding a proposed anti-abortion constitutional amendment, that "it is seldom appropriate for one group within a society to seek to insert their moral beliefs, however profoundly held, into a document designed for people of fundamentally differing views." During his long tenure on the Supreme Court, Justice William Brennan, a staunch Catholic, was one of the strongest supporters of church-state separation ever to serve on the Court.

Finally, the constitution of the predominantly Catholic Puerto Rico, adopted in 1952 and approved by Congress, states that "there shall be complete separation of church and state," and that "no public property or public funds shall be used for the support of schools or educational institutions other than those of the state."

As a student in Catholic schools in the 1940s, I never heard or saw a remark deprecating church-state separation.

❧

'War on Christmas' idea is overblown

Washington Examiner, December 21, 2005

Religious fundamentalists are insisting that the American Civil Liberties Union and "liberal plotters" are seeking to do away with Christmas. They must be living in some imagined alternate universe. The ACLU and church-state separatists have nothing against Christmas or Christians. They seek only to keep the government's hands off any religion's sacred days.

These critics should be reminded that colonial New England Puritans, spiritual ancestors of today's fundamentalists, disapproved so strongly of Christmas that they outlawed even its private celebration.

Also, Congress was officially in session on Christmas until 1856; businesses and schools remained open on Christmas until the late 1880s; Christmas was not a legal holiday in all states until near the end of the 19th century; and several mainstream Christian denominations declined to celebrate Christmas until the 20th century.

It should also be noted that a larger percentage of Americans celebrate Chrsitmas today than at any time in our history.

❧

Saudi prince should promote tolerance

Washington Examiner, December 16, 2005

Bin Talal plans to donate $20 million to Georgetown University to promote religious tolerance and understanding. The truth is that the U.S. is one of the most religiously tolerant countries in the world, while Saudi Arabia is one of the least tolerant.

In Saudi Arabia, it is illegal for a Muslim to change his religion and any non-Muslim religious observance is forbidden.

Sharia law rules, and penalties for violating it are severe.

Women are discriminated against and are not even allowed to drive cars.

Prince Alwaleed's heart may be in the right place, but his interest in religious tolerance would be better directed toward his own homeland.

∽❧

Women's Rights Come First

Washington Post, December 6, 2005

Thomas M. Doran's Nov. 27 letter on rights for the unborn ignored a woman's right to freedom of conscience and choice in dealing with problem pregnancies.

He also conflated embryonic or fetal life with human personhood, which neurobiology shows is not possible until after 28 weeks of gestation. Mr. Doran may believe as he pleases, but the notion of human personhood in the absence of a functioning cerebral cortex, before 28 to 32 weeks, has no substantial scientific, biblical, historical or "humanistic" basis.

What is of supreme importance is the right of every woman to freedom of choice.

∽❧

School Vouchers Would Fragment America

Washington Times, November 8, 2005

Nancy Salvato's "Mythology versus school choice (Forum, Sunday) conveniently overlooked important considerations.

Millions of Americas in 25 statewide referendums have rejected school vouchers or their analogues by a 2-to-1 margin.

Republican Kansas state Sen. John Vratil correctly observes that private schools accepting public funds would have to play by the same rules as public schools. As most nonpublic schools by far are faith-based institutions that commonly discriminate in admissions, directly or indirectly, along religious, class, ethnic, ability level and other lines and permeate their curricula with sectarian teaching, taxing all citizens to support them would, to a constitutional originalist, be as "sinful and tyrannical" as James Madison, main author of the First Amendment, declared in 1785 in his famous Memorial and Remonstrance Against Religious Assessments.

School vouchers would fragment our society along creedal, class, ethnic and other lines. Ben Franklin's advice that "we shall either hang together or hang separately" is certainly applicable to the controversy over school vouchers. Aren't there enough divisions in our society?

Incidentally, a 2004 statewide poll by the Baton Rouge Advocate showed that Louisianians in every part of the state opposed vouchers by a 60 percent to 34 percent margin despite the fact that the state's public schools are grossly underfunded.

ꭥ

Will Secularism Survive?

Free Inquiry, October/November 2005

When applied to government, secularism refers to neutrality toward all religions and lifestances. Thomas Jefferson and James Madison described this as "separation of church and state." In 1879, and again in 1947 and later rulings, the U.S. Supreme Court held that Jefferson and Madison clearly expressed the intent of the First Amendment.

The treaty with Tripoli, approved by the Senate and signed by President John Adams in 1797, declares that "The government of the United States of America is in no sense founded on the Christian religion." Similarly relevant is the Puerto Rican constitution's clause declaring, "There shall be complete separation of church and state," language approved by Congress in 1952 during McCarthyism's heyday.

Since the 1970s, we've seen the rise of a Religious Right composed primarily of Protestant fundamentalists (led by Pat Robertson, Jerry Falwell, James Dobson, Tim LaHaye, D. James Kennedy, etc.) and augmented by Catholic and Jewish fundamentalists. Allied with secular special interests, they've dominated the Republican Party, achieved significant power and media influence, and succeeded in advancing their pernicious agendas: eroding public education in favor of tax-supported, selective faith-based schools; reducing public welfare programs in favor of tax-supported, often discriminatory faith-based charities; using public schools to promote fundamentalist "creationism" and "abstinence-only" sexuality education; increasing restrictions on reproductive freedom; and indifference toward the global problems of overpopulation and climate change.

Will secularism survive? It will only if humanists and moderate to liberal Catholics, Protestants, Jews, and others work together. How? Through such organizations as the American Civil Liberties Union, People for the American Way, the Religious Coalition for Reproductive Choice, and Americans for Religious Liberty, among others. Further, organizations like the unique Texas Freedom Network (www.tfm.org) need to be created in every state.

Secularism will survive if we put our minds, energy, organizations, and money to work.

Another Reason to Resist Melding Public, Private

Education Week, October 26, 2005

Regarding your Oct. 12, 2005, front-page article "Catholic Schools Reopening After Katrina":

One cannot help but notice that, in the two accompanying photographs of students, only one of the dozens shown is African-American. Nearby public schools surely would have many more black faces. This lack of diversity in Catholic schools is one more reason why the Bush administration's intent to favor private schools with $488 million in public funds is not a good idea.

Public Schools Need Help, Not Destruction

Education Week, October 26, 2005

In his Oct. 12, 2005, letter to the editor, economist John Merrifield recommends "free enterprise" as the answer to Louisiana's school problems. I assume "free enterprise" is code for school vouchers.

We've been through this repeatedly in California (1982, 1993, 2000). Each time, and by ever greater margins, voters have rejected vouchers—by 71 percent to 29 percent in 2000—despite the fact that Proposition 13 has seriously damaged our public schools. The same voter rejection of vouchers by large margins has occurred in many other states, from the West Coast to the East Coast, and in states in between, including Louisiana.

Public schools are the backbone of our democracy. They need help, not destruction.

Seeing a Cynical Use of Katrina Victims' Plight

Education Week, October 19, 2005

The Bush administration's plan to allot $488 million to pay for Hurricane Katrina evacuee children to attend private, mainly faith-based schools for a year ("Relief Plans Spurring Debate Over Vouchers," Sept. 28, 2005) is a cynical, opportunistic attempt to use hurricane victims as a wedge to promote the religious right's goal of making taxpayers support discriminatory, pervasively sectarian private schools.

Louisiana citizens made clear last year in an opinion poll by *The Advocate*, Baton Rouge's newspaper, that they oppose vouchers by 60 percent to 34 percent, with opposition in every region of the state. Whites opposed vouchers by 59 percent to 35 percent, while blacks were opposed by 63 percent to 33 percent.

Federal funds for young hurricane victims should go only to public schools that are open to all and without discrimination or indoctrination. The administration's private school aid plan can only further complicate the already chaotic and inadequate responses to the terrible storms, create administrative confusion, and stir up political controversy at a time when the country needs to pull together.

The bill sponsored by U.S. Sens. Michael B. Enzi and Edward M. Kennedy, though not nearly as bad as the Bush plan, should also be rejected for many of the same reasons.

Pledge ruling could have shredded First Amendment

Washington Examiner, October 17, 2005

The *Examiner* was pretty much on target regarding the debate surrounding the Pledge of Allegiance.

Shortly before Michael Newdow argued his Pledge challenge before the Supreme Court in 2004, he and I were involved in an ACLU-sponsored debate at the University of Maryland. I made the point that he was probably right that insertion of "under God" in the Pledge of Allegiance in 1954 was unconstitutional.

However, I hastened to add that if Newdow won his case, there would surely be an unstoppable amendment to the Constitution that would shred the

First Amendment and set church-state separation and religious freedom back centuries. If he lost, the ruling would have been written by either Chief Justice William Rehnquist or Justice Clarence Thomas and the result would have been just as bad.

Fortunately, the court dismissed the case for Newdow's lack of standing.

As you wisely point out, such quixotic tilting at windmills can only distract attention from really serious threats to religious freedom and church-state separation, such as the effort to introduce religious doctrine in science classes, the endless campaign to have government force all taxpayers to support discriminatory faith-based schools through school vouchers and the equally endless drive to restrict the freedom of conscience of women in dealing with problem pregnancies.

☞

Campolo, Pro & Con

The Progressive, October 2005

John Oliver Mason's piece on Tony Campolo was refreshing ("Meet Evangelist Tony Campolo," August issue). Since evangelicals like Campolo and Jim Wallis share a great many social justice values—except, perhaps, on reproductive rights—with liberal and progressive Catholics, mainstream Protestants, Jews, humanists, secularists, and others, we all need to work more closely together to roll back the advance of rapacious secular conservatives and narrow-minded intolerant fundamentalists.

☞

Keep God out of the Pledge of Allegiance

University of South Alabama *Vanguard*, September 27, 2005

Newdow may well be right that adding "Under God" to the Pledge is unconstitutional. But, as I pointed out in a debate with him at an ACLU sponsored meeting at the University of Maryland shortly before he argued his case before the Supremes, if he won there would be an unstoppable constitutional amendment that would likely shred the First Amendment; if he lost the ruling by either Rehnquist or Thomas would be equally damaging. In defending church-state separation we have to think strategically instead of charging windmills like Don Quixote. Newdow's new effort may make him feel good, but it could well set church-state separation back centuries.

⌒⊙➔

Church and state

Washington Times, September 21, 2005

David Limbaugh's interpretation of the First Amendment is wrong ("Benchmarks of activism," Commentary, Monday).

As the records of the first Congress clearly show, First Amendment language merely to ban "establishment of a national religion," which we were in no danger of having, was specifically rejected in favor of the provision, "Congress shall make no law respecting an establishment of religion, or prohibiting the free exercise thereof." Thomas Jefferson correctly wrote in 1802 that this provision built "a wall of separation between church and state," and the Supreme Court rather faithfully agreed, from its first church-state case in 1947 until the 1990s, when the Rehnquist court began, improperly, to take bricks out of the "wall."

The Supreme Court's church-state rulings, until beginning to waver in the mid-1990s, protected and advanced the free exercise of religion and religious freedom by ending government meddling with religion.

We might note that as recently as 1952, Congress approved the constitution of the Commonwealth of Puerto Rico, which copies the First Amendment and then adds, "there shall be complete separation of church and state."

⌒⊙➔

World Without *Roe*

Christian Century, September 20, 2005

David Heim's "World without *Roe*?" (Aug. 9) was a bit cavalier. If *Roe v. Wade* goes down, there will be endless battles in Congress and state legislatures over the extent to which male solons will allow women freedom of conscience. Also, poor and young women will likely find choice inaccessible in "red" states and away from cities.

One can agree with Heim that the need for abortion can and should be reduced through comprehensive sexuality education, better access to contraceptives (including morning-after pills), universal health insurance, prosecution of predatory or abusive males, etc. But there is simply no way of getting around the question, "Who chooses, the individual woman or Big Brother government?" This is especially so as the Judeo-Christian scriptures neither mention nor condemn abortion and as modern neuroscience shows that the functions of personhood are not possible until after 28-32 weeks of gestation—a view that fits nicely with the idea that persons are "created in the image of God," which has nothing to do with flesh, bone, DNA or beating hearts.

☞

Enlightened school board

Salt Lake Tribune, September 11, 2005

The Utah Board of Education is to be commended for sticking up for science education and for rejecting appeals from religious fundamentalists to confuse students with the thinly disguised "creationism" that the U.S. Supreme Court ruled unconstitutional in 1987. Too bad that Kansas' State Board of Education is not as enlightened.

☞

Collapse Predicted in 1974

Skeptic, Vol. 11, No. 4, 2005

Thanks for excerpting Jared Diamond's important book Collapse (Vol. 11, No. 3), Though new, it concentrates and develops an overview of what many have written for perhaps 50 years, but to which too few have paid heed. Much of what Diamond has expressed alarm about is contained in a report ordered by President Nixon in 1974 and completed and approved by President Ford in 1975. The National Security Study Memorandum 200 (NSSM 200) report was titled "Implications of Worldwide Population Growth for US Security and Overseas Interests." Tragically, the report was "classified" and deep-sixed until shortly before the 1994 UN International Conference on Population and Development in Cairo. Whoever was responsible for burying this report for nearly a generation not only exacerbated the problems Diamond explores but also brought misery, sickness, and death to many millions. The hour is late, but not too late for humankind to address these problems, which will involve reining in the Religious Right, Evangelical and Muslim, and overcoming the resistance of the Bush administration.

∞

The Fuel-Cell Car

US News & World Report, August 29, 2005

Producing hydrogen for fuel-cell-powered cars need not create more pollution. Hydrogen can be produced by breaking down seawater with wind or solar power.

∞

Claims of bias at PBS are unwarranted

Washington Examiner, August 24, 2005

Regarding David Boaz's piece, while National Public Radio and PBS fall short of perfection, they are vastly superior to just about everything on the commercial electronic media and in much of the print media as well.

While each and every presentation on NPR and PBS cannot be perfectly balanced, on the whole public broadcasting is as fair and balanced as is humanly possible.

Withdrawal of the rather limited government support that public broadcasting receives would be a serious blow to a vitally important institution, and would make it much more difficult for citizens to receive good professional news coverage and all the other benefits that millions of Americans have come to be grateful for.

∞

(Untitled)

National Catholic Reporter, August 12, 2005

Regarding *NCR*'s feature "Resurrecting Mary Magdalene", Australian writer Donovan Joyce wrote in his 1973 book The Jesus Scroll (published in the UK but never in the United States) that the story of the wedding feast of Cana in John makes no sense unless Jesus was the bridegroom. He wrote that Mary Magdalene was the bride, that they had a son and that Jesus and his son died at the Roman siege of Masada.

Friedman 'Willfully Ignores' Voucher Damage

Education Week, July 27, 2005

School voucher granddaddy Milton Friedman's comments during his interview with *Education Week* ("Friedman: The Solution is Choice," www.edweek.org, June 22, 2005) show that he willfully ignores the fact that vouchers would raise schooling costs, seriously damage the teaching profession by imposing religious tests on teachers, and promote and subsidize the fragmentation of school populations along sectarian, class, ethnic, and ideological lines. They also show that he scorns the wisdom of the millions of voters who have rejected voucher plans or their analogues by two-to-one in 25 statewide referendums between 1967 and 2004, and that he scoffs at the wisdom of national and state constitution writers since 1787 who recognized that forcing taxpayers to support sectarian schools is, in Thomas Jefferson's words, "sinful and tyrannical".

One wonders what Mr. Friedman thinks of the three-to-one rejection by Newfoundland voters of their in-place universal voucher plan in the 1990s and its replacement by American-style religiously neutral public schools.

Commandments' differing versions

Maryland Gazette, July 6, 2005

The Ten Commandments display in the county's Judicial Center in Rockville may well be situated along with other historic documents, but that does not alter the fact that there is no single agreed-upon version of the Commandments ("County beat rush on Supreme Court ruling," June 29).

Thus, whichever version is displayed clearly favors some religious traditions over others and so is of questionable constitutionality.

There is no barrier to our many houses of worship displaying the Commandments, any version they choose, in their yards and interiors, or to their placement on any other private property. But government has no business favoring some religions over others.

∽❧

Intelligent Decision on 'The Privileged Planet'

Washington Post, June 8, 2005

The Smithsonian Institution is to be commended for distancing itself from the showing of "The Privileged Planet." Co-sponsorship of the creationist film would tarnish the Smithsonian's reputation in the scientific community.

The Smithsonian should consider sponsoring a program on cosmology and evolution featuring reputable, mainstream scientists.

∽❧

Iconoclash

New Republic, May 16, 2005

Jeffrey Rosen's otherwise cogent piece missed an important point: Leaving aside their Judeo-Christian heritage, there is no single agreed-upon version of the Ten Commandments, which means that any government-sponsored commandments display amounts to government preference of some faiths over others ("Big Ten," March 14). If some religious bodies and leaders are so keen on seeing the Big Ten displayed, there is nothing to stop them from doing so on the interior and exterior walls of houses of worship and other private properties. Finally, too little notice is made of the 1796-1797 Washington/Adams treaty with Tripoli, ratified by the Senate, which states that "the government of the United States of America is not in any sense founded on the Christian religion."

∽❧

Filibuster needed to restore fairness

Washington Examiner, May 4, 2005

Your editorial on the filibuster overlooked the fact that while American voters are split almost exactly 50/50 between Democrats and Republicans, thanks to the way the constitution set up the Senate so that small states could balance large states, Republicans have 55 seats. In an imperfect world, then, the filibuster of judicial appointments is a form of check and balance.

Since President Bush has made no effort to get the Democrats' advice, which represents half of the voters, it is legitimate for Senate Democrats to use the instrument of the filibuster to keep some semblance of balance in our government. If the shoe were on the other foot, the Republicans would surely do the same.

A president who came into office in 2000 as a minority candidate should be gracious enough to be less partisan and divisive.

Examiner: Reasonable points. But don't you think Democrats who say changing the filibuster is unconstitutional are just a bit hypocritical since they've already changed it twice?

Democrats may have changed the filibuster rule in the past but they did not abolish it, as Sen. Frist is considering. Without the filibuster we would have one-party government in a nation that is pretty much split down the middle.

∞

Letters by Gender

The Nation, May 2, 2005

Re Katha Pollitt's "Invisible Women" ["Subject to Debate," April 4]: Last fall I tabulated by gender the letters to the editor in the *New York Times*, the *Washington Post* and the *Washington Times*—529 letters over nineteen days. The percentages of writers, by gender: 73 percent by men, 27 percent by women. The breakdown for women by paper was: *New York Times*, 31 percent; *Washington Post*, 26 percent; *Washington Times*, 15 percent. The study was hardly scientific, but it showed that the number of letters by women was related to how liberal the paper is.

∞

Sen. Salazar is right to criticize religious groups

Washington Examiner, April 27, 2005

Sen. Ken Salazar, D-Colo., is right in criticizing Focus on the Family and similar groups for seeking to use the Republican Party to turn the United States into a fundamentalist theocracy, as if the world didn't already have enough of them. This movement, which threatens the religious freedom of all Americans, is wrong for a nation with our tremendous religious diversity, a nation whose founders invented the principle of separation of church and state.

Examiner: Perhaps Focus on the Family's statements are silly, but no more silly than the claim that they want to found a "fundamentalist theocracy." Religious people have a right to their beliefs and to use politics as a means of expressing those beliefs. Responding to them with unreasoning hyperbole won't persuade very many of them that they're wrong.

Focus on the Family's statements are not merely "silly" but dangerous, as they represent a movement of growing power and influence clearly promoting a theocratic agenda antithetical to our church-state separation tradition, an agenda that includes compelling taxpayers to support discriminatory faith-based schools and charities, weakening science education, and eroding the rights of women on reproductive matters, not to mention stacking the courts. As a lifelong church member, I consider this growing mixture of religion and politics a serious misuse of religion.

☞

Diversity among atheists

National Catholic Reporter, April 15, 2005

Brian Brennan's piece "Atheism is its own belief system" (*NCR*, March 25), though informative, was a bit oversimplified. There is as much diversity among atheists as among Christians.

There are outspoken atheists, frequently intolerant and obnoxious, who "affirm the absence of God." But there are far more "nontheists"—who may refer to themselves as agnostics, humanists, Unitarians, humanistic Jews, etc.— who would say that among the many things not included in their belief systems are a deity, a supernatural order or leprechauns. Just as Catholics do not include in their belief system reincarnation, predestination or zombies.

Just as there are Ayn Rand-type Libertarian atheists, there are vastly more moderate to progressive nontheists who share many important values with moderate to progressive Catholics, Protestants and Jews.

Finally, the word "disbelief" is rather useless. Everyone has a set of beliefs, and everyone is a "disbeliever" in whatever conflicts with one's beliefs.

Moderate to progressive Catholics, Protestants, Jews and nontheists have much more in common than any of them have with either religious or atheistic fundamentalists.

☞

Church-State Comments on Three Recent Stories

Education Week, March 30, 2005

Three articles in your March 9, 2005, issue merit comment:

First, there is an upside to the precipitous decline of Roman Catholic school enrollment over the last 40 years, from 50 percent of Catholic kids to fewer than 20 percent ("Catholic Schools' Mission to Serve Needy Children Jeopardized by Closings"). Transfers to public schools strengthen public education, make available additional teachers for public schools, and should increase political support for more adequate funding for public schools.

Second, Utah's passage of a school voucher bill "Special-Needs Vouchers Pass Utah House, Senate") not only violates the state constitution but also runs counter to the expressed wishes of Utah voters, who in 1988 rejected a tax-code voucher scheme by 70 percent to 30 percent.

Third, Andrew Coulson's recommendation of "school choice," meaning vouchers, as a way out of the evolution/creationism problem ("Ending the Evolutionary War," Commentary) is no solution at all, for two reasons: Scientists are virtually unanimous in insisting that evolution is the indispensable core of biology, geology, and astrophysics and must not be compromised by being confused with the "intelligent design" idea that has no scientific support.

And, as a Michigan resident, Mr. Coulson should know that his state's voters rejected tax-supported "school choice" at the polls three times: in 1970 by 57 percent to 43 percent, in 1978 by 74 percent to 26 percent, and in 2000 by 69 percent to 31 percent.

On such stories as these, I think it would be good journalism to present contrasting points of view. Nonetheless, *Education Week* is an indispensable publication.

Voucher Plan Disregards Wishes of D.C. Voters

Education Week, March 16, 2005

Sally Sacher's letter defending the District of Columbia school voucher plan ("Key Facts Overlooked in Voucher-Program Report," Letters, march 2, 2005) overlooked an important fact: The plan was imposed on the District of Columbia by Congress against the wishes of the majority of Washington residents.

When local voters had a chance to vote on a tax-code voucher plan in 1981, they rejected it 89 percent to 11 percent.

No school voucher plan has ever been approved by a state's voters. The Wisconsin, Ohio, Florida, and District of Columbia voucher plans were adopted not by the people, but by political fiat.

Furthermore, Gov. Jeb Bush of Florida's new attempt to promote vouchers in his state, while the matter is still before the state supreme court, shows contempt for that court and for his state's constitution.

No fan of Judge Bork

Washington Times, March 13, 2005

Bruce Fein's enthusiasm for nominating "undiluted Borks to the Supreme Court" ("Embedded message," Commentary, Tuesday), is a bit much.

Before Judge Robert H. Bork was nominated, I heard him address a huge audience at the Washington Hilton. The core of his message: Permanent or temporary majorities have the right to impose their beliefs and values on minorities. Immediately after he was nominated to the Supreme Court, I was one of the journalists who spent a day reading the papers Judge Bork had turned over to the Senate Judiciary Committee. I found little evidence of his much-heralded brilliance but much of his odd obsessions.

In the succeeding weeks, I appeared on at least 30 talk shows, making the point that the Senate should approve only those who are enthusiastic supporters of the Bill of Rights.

Much to Learn from Newfoundland

Phi Delta Kappan, March 2005

With regard to "Friendly Fire," Heather-jane Robertson's November in Canada column, it is clear that we in the U.S. can learn much from our neighbor to the north, whose inhabitants are sometimes referred to as "English-speaking Scandinavians."

The case of Newfoundland/Labrador, in area about the size of Washington and Oregon combined and in population similar to Vermont, is an interesting one. The province had no public schools, only several groups of tax-supported faith-based schools that reportedly constituted the worst school system in Canada. Then in the mid-1990s, the province's voters decided by a 3-to-1 margin to scrap the old system and convert to U.S.-style religiously neutral public schools. In essence, Newfoundland/Labrador once had a sort of universal voucher plan, the kind of idea that some conservatives and sectarian special interests are working feverishly to promote here in the U.S., despite being repeatedly rebuffed at the ballot box. Will Americans profit from Newfoundland's experience?

Having converted rapidly to a public school system, Newfoundland/Labrador then moved to create curricula for teaching "about" religion in a fair, inclusive, and balanced way. A series of texts for grades 4-6—"Journeys," "Directions," and "Horizons"—introduce children through age-appropriate narratives to Christianity, Judaism, Islam, Jainism, Buddhism, Sikhism, Baha'i, and aboriginal Canadian religions. *Who Am I?* and *My Place in the World,* the eighth- and ninth-grade texts (I haven't seen the seventh-grade text), move on to sophisticated discussions of social and ethical problems and how different religious traditions, including the "unchurched," deal with them. Among the topics covered are how values and personal identity develop; friendship, love, commitment, and sexuality; HIV and AIDS; social justice; racism; culture shock; immigration; the environment and ecology; changing moral standards, science, and religion; cloning and in-vitro fertilization; interfaith dialogue; and globalization.

These texts, from one of Canada's poorest and most sparsely populated provinces, could be profitably emulated in the U.S. Needless to say, they are undoubtedly too sophisticated and "liberal" to ever be adopted in many of our states. Yes, there is much to be learned from our Canadian friends.

Tuition waiver for Scouts would be discriminatory

Howard County (MD) *News*, February 24, 2005

House Bill 296 would provide college tuition waivers for Eagle Scouts and Girl Scout Gold Awardees. It should be defeated because it would invidiously discriminate against students who for religious, financial or other reasons won't or can't get into the Scouts. If the state has any extra money to throw around it should be used to aid students in financial need.

Not enough women in Congress or legislatures

Washington Examiner, February 23, 2005

I've long noticed that there are more letters to the editor published from men than women. So last fall, I tabulated all the letters published in *The New York Times, The Washington Post,* and *The Washington Times* for 19 days.

The result: Out of a total of 529 letters, only 27 percent were from women.

A further breakdown by paper showed that 31 percent of the letters in the NY Times were from women, 26 percent in the Post and 16 percent in the Washington Times. Though this survey was hardly scientific, it seems to show that the more liberal the paper, the more women get published.

Women are certainly as intelligent as men, so one wonders if there would be more gender balance if they were as assertive. (A testosterone thing?)

If women were proportionately represented in Congress and state legislatures, we would have a different—and probably better—country.

Focus on Dobson

US News & World Report, February 14, 2005

James Dobson's plunge into politics is the sort of mixture of religion and politics that Thomas Jefferson and James Madison warned against more than two centuries ago. Dobson may spend "only" 6 percent of his $146 million budget directly on influencing public policy, but $8.76 million can pay for a lot of influence.

☞

Planned Parenthood Facts

National Catholic Reporter, February 4, 2005

John Naughton's attack on Planned Parenthood (letters, *NCR*, Jan. 14) was woefully short on facts. Allow me to correct him.

Many Planned Parenthood facilities are located in poor areas, many of them African-American, because upper-middle-class people have little need of their services.

No federal funds are used by Planned Parenthood for abortions. And in Mr. Naughton's state of Maryland, of the 36,000 patients seen by Planned Parenthood last year only 3,100 were for terminating pregnancies. Much of Planned Parenthood's work is providing prenatal and fertility counseling in addition to providing family planning assistance to those, married or unmarried, who want it.

Planned Parenthood's goal is a world of wanted and adequately cared-for children.

Alleviating or eliminating poverty, misery and their effects, both here and abroad, is something that all of us, Catholics and non-Catholics alike, should be working on. The mere pittance of public and private funding that is expended for family planning, which polls show most Catholics favor, is insignificant compared to the needs of the poor.

People like Mr. Naughton can't seem to see the forest for the trees.

☞

Pledge Lawsuit Seen as 'Quixotic' Diversion

Education Week, February 2, 2005

Michael A. Newdow may well be right that Congress' insertion of "under God" in the Pledge of Allegiance is unconstitutional ("New Challenge to Pledge in Schools Filed," Jan. 12, 2005), but his quixotic lawsuit challenging it may be less a kamikaze mission than a Götterdämmerung: If he wins, the country will surely face an unstoppable constitutional amendment that would likely shred the First Amendment. If he loses, the language of the ruling could be equally damaging to church-state separation. As in every struggle, strategy is all-important.

I pointed this out in a debate with him at an American Civil Liberties Union-sponsored affair at the University of Maryland last spring.

Defenders of religious freedom would more usefully spend their time and effort working to stop the diversion of public funds to faith-based nonpublic schools and obtain more adequate funding for our public schools.

∽❥

Column on religion 'staggeringly naive'

Maryland Journal, January 24, 2005

Karen Hart's January 18 column on religion and government ("What would Washington do?") was staggeringly naive.

She seems unaware that our country's central founding document—the Constitution—does not mention a deity, while the Bill of Rights provides for separation of religion and government.

Hart wonders why "we don't want prayer in school." Who doesn't? Kids are free to pray in school every day. The law only prohibits government mandated or sponsored prayer.

She also wonders why the Ten Commandments cannot be displayed in a courthouse, seemingly unaware that there is no agreed upon version of the Commandments. Why, one might ask, aren't the Ten Commandments prominently displayed on—and in—our churches?

Her mention of the religious motto "In God We Trust" on our money is oblivious to the fact that it did not begin to be on our coinage until the Civil War, or on our currency until after World War II.

Yes, the Declaration of Independence mentions "nature's God"—to rally people against a powerful empire based on the divine right of kings. How better to counter that than by asserting the divine rights of the people?

Once independent, though, we dropped such references from the Constitution.

Ms. Hart views all religion as rosy and wonderful. Is she really unaware that religion has been used to defend slavery and segregation, persecution and bigotry, anti-Semitism and anti-Catholicism, homophobia and racism, denial of rights to women, colonialism and indifference to the plight of the oppressed?

Some manifestations of religion are good and some are bad. We need to be able to tell the difference—and also to continue to uphold the principle of separation of church and state that safeguards the religious freedom of all.

❦

Established Science vs. Philosophical Speculation

Education Week, January 19, 2005

Christopher Gieschen's rather confused letter ("Approach to Evolution Depends on 'Worldview'," Letters, Jan. 5, 2005) suggests something like parity between evolution, which is well-established science, and "intelligent design" creationism, which is almost entirely religious or philosophical speculation/ opinion, lacking any scientific support.

Students and adults are free to accept scientific conclusions or to prefer any of a wide variety of nonscientific religious explanations of natural phenomena or, as a very great many do, to accept science and accommodate their religious views to the conclusions of science. But what public schools may not do, as the U.S. Supreme Court made clear in 1987, is mix religious explanations into science classes.

❦

Get Used to 'Under God'

New York Times, January 13, 2005

Re "Atheist Files Second suit on 'Under God' in Pledge" (news article, Jan. 6):

Although Congress's 1954 insertion of the phrase "under God" into the Pledge of Allegiance is of doubtful constitutionality, Michael Newdow's attempts to have the courts remove the phrase are unwise, as I pointed out in a debate with him last spring (at an A.C.L.U.-sponsored meeting at the University of Maryland).

Should he win in the Supreme Court, the country's response would surely be an unstoppable constitutional amendment that could well shred the First

Amendment. Should he lose, the ruling would likely also damage the First Amendment.

Defenders of religious freedom and church-state separation should expend their effort on more important issues, such as blocking efforts to force all taxpayers to support faith-based schools or to impose faith-based limits on reproductive freedom.

☞

Pope should talk about 'arrogance of power'

Maryland Journal, January 13, 2005

On Jan. 10, Pope John Paul II criticized the "arrogance of power," adding that "it is necessary that religious freedom be everywhere provided with an effective constitutional guarantee."

So far, so good. But the pope hastened to add that religious freedom does not include the right of all persons to freedom of conscience regarding reproduction or embryonic stem cell research.

He also has a history of opposing the right of citizens not to be forced by government to involuntarily contribute to the support of religious institutions.

And speaking of the arrogance of power, John Paul's church is the only one in the world that enjoys "permanent observer" status at the United Nations General Assembly, a position that it uses to work against women's rights and efforts to deal with the overpopulation problem.

Most Catholics disagree with his positions on these issues, but have no voice in their church to do anything about it.

☞

A Little Texas Barbecue

The Nation, January 10/17, 2005

In addition to the Western election bright spots cited by John Nichols ["Democrats Score in the Rockies," Dec. 6], we might note these: Voters in Bush's own Texas district re-elected embattled Congressman Chet Edwards, a Democrat with a strong church-state separation record. And South Dakota voters, while boosting Bush and dashing Daschle, also defeated a referendum proposal to provide tax aid to faith-based schools—and did so most strongly in those counties that went big for Bush. That brings to twenty-six the number of statewide referendums between 1966 and 2004 in which voters rejected tax aid to faith-based schools by an average margin of two to one.

Christians have very high visibility

Maryland Journal, January 4, 2005

In her Dec. 31 letter ("When did Christians lose their rights?") Jan Bise claims that Christians are "losing the religious rights guaranteed by our Constitution."

Such a serious charge should be backed up with evidence or examples, not merely some vague, absurd claim about being told she cannot "publicly display the fact that [she] believes in Christ."

Our country has 2,000 radio and TV stations owned mainly by evangelicals. There are more Christian bookstores and book racks in supermarkets than there are gas stations. There are hundreds of thousands of houses of worship.

And about 85 percent of the U.S. population professes Christianity, as do more than 90 percent of members of Congress.

What if?

Washington Times, January 4, 2005

Thanks for running the article "Spanish Civil War victims speak out" (World, Sunday). If the United States, the United Kingdom and France had come to the defense of the elected Spanish Republican government in 1936, as Adolf Hitler and Benito Mussolini rushed to help Gen. Francisco Franco's rebellion, the Nazis might not have been able to start World War II, Josef Stalin would not have had time to stick his nose into the matter, and today's world would be a far different and probably better place.

Scientists support theory of evolution

Baltimore Sun, January 1, 2005

The writer of the letter "Many scientists still skeptical about evolution" (Dec. 27) is wrong in saying that there is "significant disagreement among qualified scientists as to the feasibility of the theory of evolution."

There is virtually no disagreement. The National Academy of Sciences, the American Anthropological Association, the American Association for the Advancement of Science, the American Chemical Society, the American Geological Institute, the American Physical Society, the American Society of Biological Chemists and the National Association of Biology Teachers are among the many top science organizations that agree that evolution is a well-established central principle of science.

As the National Academy of Sciences has put it: "It is . . . our unequivocal conclusion that creationism, with its account of the origin of life by supernatural means, is not science. It subordinates science to statements based on authority and revelation. . . . No body of beliefs that has its origin in doctrinal material rather than scientific observation should be admissible as science in any science course."

Religion and science need not compete on the same ground, and all people are free to believe as they please.

But in the field of education, theology cannot be allowed to trump science.

☞

Long history of church-state separation

Maryland Journal, December 28, 2004

In his Dec. 23 letter, Michael Pearce claims that the "wall of separation [between] church and state" did not "come into being until 1964" ("Christmas displays should be allowed"). Wrong!

Church-state separation is implied in the Constitution (1787) by its refusal to authorize government to mess with religion, and made more explicit in the First amendment (1789).

In 1802, President Thomas Jefferson, with the backing of Attorney General Levi Lincoln, declared that the First Amendment "built a wall of separation between church and state."

In 1879, the Supreme Court held that Jefferson's statement "may be accepted almost as an authoritative declaration of the scope and effect" of the

First Amendment (Reynolds v. United States).

Beginning in 1947, the Supreme Court began a solid series of rulings upholding church-state separation.

In 1952, Congress approved the constitution for the commonwealth of Puerto Rico, which states that "There shall be complete separation of church and state."

Nearly every state constitution contains language asserting that principle.

For more than 200 years, most religious leaders have agreed that church-state separation is vital to preserve religious freedom for all. The danger to religious freedom today is that President George W. Bush will try to appoint Supreme Court justices like Clarence Thomas and Antonin Scalia who have shown contempt for this basic constitutional principle.

As for Christmas displays, it should be noted that Christmas was largely frowned upon and illegal in colonial New England, that most Protestant churches did not celebrate Christmas until late in the 19th century (and some still do not), and that Congress itself was officially in session on Christmas until 1856.

An excellent history of Christmas observance is Montgomery County author Albert Menendez' book, *The December Wars*.

∽❧

Public policy supports abortion

Maryland Journal, December 20, 2004

Lawrence Marsh is right that polls do not determine what is right and wrong ("Respecting our freedom of conscience," Dec. 15), but on the other hand, polls, elections, referenda and legislative procedures do determine public policy.

If public policy determines that poor women are entitled to a full range of tax-paid health care, then it would be unfair for the state to say that Mary is entitled to a tax-paid Caesarian section but Susie is not entitled to a tubal ligation or a first-trimester abortion just because Mr. Marsh and others regard it as sinful.

There is universal consensus against murder, the intentional killing of another person for reasons other than self-defense.

But what is a person? Under U.S. law, a person is someone born. Therefore, a fetus is not a person.

Modern neurobiology shows that the functions associated with personhood are not possible until some time after 28 weeks of gestation—a view that to many coincides with the notion that persons "are created in the image of God," which of course has nothing to do with flesh, bone or DNA.

What about the Bible? It does not mention abortion. The Hebrew scriptures (what Christians call the Old Testament) define a person as something that has been born ("nefesh").

All of us who are "pro-life" and also pro-freedom of conscience should be working to see that all children in the world have an adequate living standard, that all women have total equality with men and that violence in the settlement of disputes is minimized.

∞

Taxes shouldn't support war in Iraq

Maryland Journal, December 9, 2004

Lawrence Marsh dug himself into a couple of holes in his Dec. 7 letter to the editor ("Taxes shouldn't support abortion either").

First, if "it is tyranny for government to use taxpayer money to support a practice that millions of Americans find repulsive and immoral" as he writes, then our government logically should not be using our tax money to support a war/occupation in Iraq that many millions of Americans believe is "repulsive and immoral."

Second, Mr. Marsh declares that "abortion is clearly an anti-God practice."

While he has a right to this personal opinion, he nonetheless impugns the faith and morals of the many millions of Americans who believe that terminating problem pregnancies is either always—or often—a morally acceptable choice.

This is a view held by many millions of people of faith who support the Religious Coalition for Reproductive Rights, which directly represents 40 Protestant, Catholic, Jewish and other faith groups.

He might also recall that in 1992, a strong majority of Marylanders voted to uphold the right of all women to freedom of reproductive choice.

∞

Instead of gifts, why not feed the hungry?

Maryland Journal, December 7, 2004

Has anyone ever calculated how much people spend each year for outdoor Christmas lights and decorations? Or for whole forests of pine trees that will be trashed in January?

Or for unwanted and unneeded gifts?

Wouldn't it make more sense if all that money were spent feeding the hungry, sheltering the homeless, providing medical care for the uninsured poor, tutoring disadvantaged kids and relieving poverty and misery in the Third World?

Where are people's priorities?

Taxes shouldn't support religious charities

Maryland Journal, December 3, 2004

Your Nov. 30 editorial on faith-based programs properly expressed support for a "solid wall" of separation between church and state, but then voiced support for President Bush's "faith-based" initiative—without noting that Bush intends that civil rights regulations not be applied to these recipients of public funding ("No leap needed with faith-based programs").

Faith-based institutions have certainly made important contributions to the welfare of many, but should they be supported by taxpayers?

We would do well to remember the sound advice offered by Benjamin Franklin in his "Poor Richard's Almanack" exactly 250 years ago.

He wrote: "When a religion is good, I conceive it will support itself; and when it does not support itself, and God does not care to support it, so that its adherents are obliged to call for the help of the government, 'tis a sign, I think, of its being a bad one . . . God helps them that help themselves."

Donations to faith-based charities are tax-deductible. That is enough government aid.

Public funds should be confined to institutions responsible—and accountable—to the taxpaying public.

Tax support for sectarian charities weakens the willingness of people to support religious institutions voluntarily.

S.D. Is Latest to Reject Aid for Private Schools

Education Week, November 24, 2004

You provided excellent coverage of the state ballot measures before voters this past Nov. 2. You reported South Dakota's referendum defeat of Amendment B, which would have authorized some limited forms of tax aid for faith-based schools. But there is more to the story ("Ballot Measures," Table, Nov. 10, 2004).

The measure failed by 53 percent to 47 percent and was rejected in 56 of the state's 66 counties. It lost by 51 percent to 49 percent in the state's two largest cities, and by 54 percent to 46 percent in small towns and rural areas. In the dozen counties in which President Bush received his highest vote, 59.4 percent rejected the amendment. In Lawrence County, which last voted for a Democrat for president in 1916, 57 percent turned the measure down. In the three counties with the highest nonpublic school enrollment (Brule, 20 percent; Hand, 16 percent; Potter, 15 percent), the amendment went down 61 percent, 62 percent, and 63 percent, respectively.

The South Dakota referendum means that between 1966 and 2004, state-wide electorates in 26 referendum elections from coast to coast defeated attempts to authorize tax aid to faith-based and other private schools, through vouchers or other methods, and did so by an average ratio of 2-to-1.

It should be clear by now that Americans do not want their tax dollars going to nonpublic schools, which tend to discriminate in admissions and hiring and to be pervasively sectarian. Politicians in Washington and state capitals should move away from this idea and concentrate on providing more adequate and more equitably distributed support for our indispensable public schools.

∽❖

Does TM belong in schools?

Washington Times, November 9, 2004

Regarding the story on Transcendental Meditation (TM) in public schools ("Transcendental meditation a religious issue? Religion, Saturday), it should be noted that in the 1970s the U.S. Third Circuit Court of Appeals ruled in Malnak v. Yogi that TM is substantially religious, specifically Hindu, and therefore may not constitutionally be taught or promoted in public schools. I was one of the first researchers to call attention to TM's inescapably religious nature.

At least one public school in the District, Fletcher-Johnson, is using TM. This practice should be halted immediately, both for constitutional reasons and because it is probably costing the District money that is needed elsewhere.

Many therapists and counselors and their books (such as Dr. Herbert Benson's "The Relaxation Response") recognize the benefits of meditation for reducing stress and high blood pressure, but anyone can learn how to meditate in several different ways without resorting to the mumbo-jumbo of TM.

Appendix I

A Response to Milton Friedman

Economist Milton Friedman died on November 16, 2006, at age 94. I had the honor of being attacked by him in a letter in Education Week *on September 14, 2005. Following is a response to Friedman's attack by Louis Cable of Lufkin, Texas.*

Reader to Friedman: Stick to Economics

Milton Friedman's Sept. 14, 2005, letter slamming Edd Doerr's earlier letter on school vouchers (July 27, 2005) shows that the noted economist is out of touch with reality.

Vouchers would raise schooling costs. Religious schools, with 90 percent of the nonpublic enrollment, operate more cheaply because they do not have to serve kids with special needs. Further, really good private schools are so expensive ($14,000-plus in tuition per year) that a voucher worth about half the money spent in public schools would not get voucher students in the door, even if they could get through the schools' admissions systems. Mr. Friedman's "school choice" dream also would require a vast expansion of tax-paid transportation. Where will the money come from?

Vouchers would also "damage the teaching profession by imposing religious tests on teachers," as Mr. Doerr argues. Every study of faith-based schools, which make up 90 percent of nonpublic schools, shows that the vast majority are pervasively sectarian. A fundamentalist school is unlikely to hire a Jewish or Catholic teacher, who wouldn't want to apply to teach there anyway. The same would be true for other faith-based schools.

Vouchers clearly would divide children along sectarian, class, ethnic, and ideological lines, for financial reasons and because of the religious indoctrination prevalent in faith-based schools. Catholic kids won't be sent to fundamentalist or Muslim or Jewish schools.

Of course our public schools have problems. That is because we as a people are too cheap to provide sufficient resources to repair or replace outworn schoolbuildings and offer prekindergarten programs, especially for poor kids, and we don't distribute funding equitably among urban, suburban, and rural schools.

Mr. Friedman may know a lot about economics, but he knows precious little about education in the real world.

Appendix II

'Unbelief and Its Discontents"

As this book was being readied to go to the printer, the following letter was published in the New York Times *on November 30, 2006. As it elicited more responses, nearly all of them favorable, than any letter I've ever had published, I felt impelled to include it in this anthology. It was written in response to an op ed piece entitled "Atheists Agonistes" by Richard Shweder published in the* Times *on November 27.*

'Unbelief and its discontents'

Just as there are obnoxious Protestant, Catholic, Muslim and other fundamentalists at one end of the spectrum, so too are there obnoxious atheists at the other.

Those atheists misidentify all religious people as ignorant fundamentalists, disdain all religion, regard Unitarians and agnostics as wusses, and place the promotion of atheism ahead of any other interest.

The reality is that there is a vast middle ground of moderate to progressive Catholics, Protestants, Jews, Muslims, humanists and others who share a wide spectrum of values: protecting democracy, civil liberties, civil rights, women's rights, the environment, planetary sustainability; working for peace; ending poverty, colonialism, racism, homophobia, the growing gap between rich and poor nationally and globally.

It is important that the vast middle keep both extremes at arm's length and work together on what is important to all of us and our children and grandchildren.

Appendix III

Book Reviews

Not in Our Classrooms: Why Intelligent Design is Wrong for Our Schools, edited by Eugenie C. Scott and Glenn Branch (Beacon Press, 2006, 171 pp., $14.00).

It is more than a little disturbing that the US brings up last in the whole industrial world in acceptance of evolution. This is due to the growing strength of US fundamentalism and the weakness of school science education. A strong, fanatical anti-evolution movement is pitted against relatively scattered and un-prepared opposition, a situation not duplicated in any other advanced country.

Fortunately, in *Not in Our Classrooms* Beacon Press has provided the indispensable tool for combating this grave threat to science and science educa-tion. In this concise, lucid, compact book the authors explain what "intelligent design" (ID) creationism is all about, what is wrong with it, who is behind it, and how they operate. The authors present the scientific, theological, and legal objections to ID creationism, plus a superb chapter on precisely how to combat this threat to education.

This important book cannot be recommended too highly.

Among the juicy tidbits in the book: Sen. Rick Santorum tried unsuccess-fully to insert pro-creationism language in federal legislation, provided by ID legal theorist Philip Johnson; on November 7 Santorum was thrown out of the Senate by a landslide. In a creationist article an author asks "Would God have known that man would eventually try to explain life in evolutionary terms?"; so much for divine omniscience! Huston Smith, author of a popular college text on world religions, supports teaching ID in public schools; what can one expect from an "expert" whose textbook fails to differentiate between the liberal United Church of Christ and the conservative Church of Christ?

(Disclosure: Several years ago I was asked to respond to an address deliv-ered by Smith at a Unitarian church in Virginia. The gist of Smith's speech was that all religion can be divided into four vertical pillars, from best to worst: mysticism, polytheism, monotheism, and naturalism. My response was that his pillar idea was nonsense, that the real division in religion is a horizontal polar one. Toward one pole are progressive Christians, Jews, humanists, and others who share liberal values and are happy collaborating, while toward the other pole are various types of fundamentalists – Protestant, Catholic, Jewish, secular [sic!] who don't particularly fit well together but who share regressive goals and values.)

A terrific companion to *Not in Our Classrooms* is Eugenie Scott's *Evolution vs. Creationism: An Introduction* (Greenwood Press, 2004, 272 pp).

* * *

Contra Bush [Against Bush], by Carlos Fuentes (Aguilar, Mexico City, 2004, 159 pp., $14.95 [Border's]).

Mexican novelist/essayist Carlos Fuentes is a world class writer, pundit, and commentator, certainly worthy of a Nobel. As a speaker in English he makes George W. Bush sound like a retarded third-grader.

It's a bloody shame that this book was not published in English. It would certainly have deepened and enlivened political discussion in this country. Dedicated to Arthur Schlesinger Jr., it consists of written reflections on US politics from August 2000 through June 2004. As it does not lend itself to a regular review and is available only in Spanish, I have chosen to simply provide some pertinent quotes:

November 24, 2000: "At a dinner with Gabriel García Márquez and Bernardo Sepúlveda I asked President Clinton who were his worst enemies. 'The extreme fundamentalist right,' he replied without hesitation."

November 24, 2000: "John Ashcroft has been the most rabid enemy of abortion, gays, and feminists. He's the favorite son of Bob Jones University, which specializes in fighting interracial marriage."

February 25, 2001: "Bush has denied technical or financial aid to any foreign health organization that approves of abortion. He has endangered church-state separation and opened the coffers of public funds to churches. He is clear about his opposition to protecting the ecology and the preservation of natural areas against oil exploitation so avidly sought by his partner and vice-president Dick Cheney, former executive of the most powerful oil company in the world, Halliburton."

April 18, 2001: "The worst international decision of the younger Bush was to renounce the Kyoto Protocol against emission of global warming gases."

April 18, 2001: " . . . the puppet in the White House and his ventriloquists. . . . Where are you, Bill Clinton, when we need you so much."

December 2, 2001: "Both [Saddam Hussein and Bin Laden] are creatures of US diplomacy. Hussein, to serve Washington against the Iran of the ayatollahs. Bin Laden, to help the U.S. against the Soviet occupation of Afghanistan."

January 2, 2002: "Isn't it terrorism of another sort to deny rights to women, protection for the aged, education for kids, respect for race, creed, or sexual orientation?"

January 2, 2002: "How is it possible that in a world said to be globalized, things can circulate freely while human beings cannot?"

August 7, 2002: "In 1982 Ronald Reagan decided to secretly arm Saddam. As this was prohibited by law, he employed the indirect ways of Egypt, Jordan and Kuwait to keep the tyrant of Iraq well supplied with arms. Mrs. Thatcher [did likewise]."

August 7, 2002: "Has [Bush] thought seriously about who will govern Iraq, who will pacify Iraq, who will insure Iraq's integrity?"

September 6, 2002: "Condolleeza Rice, the Lady Macbeth of Bush's cabinet. . . ."

September 6, 2002: "Are we attending a tragic theater of Texans in which the Bush dynasty confronts itself, with Bush Jr. and his little china soldiers and cabinet – Cheney, Ashcroft, Rumsfeld, Perle – who have never faced a machine gun, opposed to the advice of Bush Sr. and his advisers experienced on real battlefields, not paper ones – Generals Powell and Schwarzkopf – or conscious of the consequences of a military action without diplomatic backing or legal basis – Baker, Scowcroft?"

September 27, 2002: "Bush Jr. has declared that 'the U.S. is the only surviving model of human progress'."

June 14, 2004: "Richard Clarke, in his celebrated book, lists a rosary of catastrophes. The US, he says, has converted Iraq into a sanctuary of terror and a reserve of Islamic rancor toward the United States. After Iraq, Al Qaeda will be neither the only nor the major Islamic terrorist group. There are now dozens of independent groups."

Remember that all of the above was written before Bush's reelection in 2004.

Oh, that we had commentators like Fuentes on TV every night.

Even if your knowledge of Spanish is weak, Fuentes writes so clearly that the reader should have little trouble.

These reviews were published in the December 2006 issue of Human Interest, *the newsletter of the Humanist Association of the Greater Sacramento Area.*

Appendix IV

Harry and Homer

Harry was no great fan of art galleries and museums, with the exception of aircraft museums. He loved the Smithsonian's Air and Space Museum and its new annex at Dulles International Airport, with its space shuttle, B-29, Corsair, P-40, and other gems. During his busy travel schedule he managed to visit air museums in Dallas, Indianapolis, and Miami.

He especially loved air shows, like the ones in Frederick, Maryland, where he once had the chance to climb into a B-17 (only 19-year-old kids could climb into the damned things, which was smaller on the inside than it appears on the outside), a Heinkel 111 (the German plane that bombed London early in World War II, with its almost harmless-looking little machinegun at the rear of the cabin), and a Junkers 52 (the ubiquitous tri-motor transport used throughout the war and which was featured in Leni Riefenstahl's 1935 propaganda documentary film, "Triumph of the Will," about Hitler's Nuremberg rally.

One of Harry's hobbies was collecting die-cast models (almost all made, and made well, in China) of aircraft, military and civilian, used from 1914 to 1945. Post-1945 planes seemed to look so much alike that they didn't interest him. Perhaps it was due to growing up in the 1930s and 1940s reading kids books about "Tailspin Tommy" and the World War I adventures of fighter pilot Phineas Pinkham at Bar le Duc (Barley Duck) airdrome in France in *Flying Aces* magazine. His hundred or so model planes all cost under $20 or he would have felt guilty about buying them.

Harry also enjoyed weekend drives to the Flying Circus in Virginia, about an hour south of Washington, to watch the air shows featuring Stearman and Waco biplanes from the 1930s. For a reasonable price he could fly around the Virginia countryside for half an hour in the front cockpit of a Stearman with the wind rushing past at eighty miles an hour. He loved the way the Stearman would leap swiftly into the air and land as gently as a feather. It was so much more enjoyable than the big impersonal jets on which he had to spend two or three or six hours at a time flying around the United States or to Europe.

But as I said, Harry was bored by most museums and art galleries. Of course, he liked the work of Velasquez, Dalí, Goya, Kandinsky, the melancholy Hopper and a few others and only collected books with the work of Hokusai, Hiroshiga, and especially that of their twentieth century successor, Kawase Hasui. He never tired of spending an hour or so with the remarkable woodblock prints by Hasui in *Visions of Japan*. He went to galleries and museums only when he was entertaining out-of-town visitors and of course Washington offered more than enough. He would let his guests wander about alone, as he hated to be tied to them, and roamed about to see only what struck his fancy.

One particular weekend the National Gallery had an exhibit of the work of nineteenth century American painter Winslow Homer. Harry was slightly acquainted with Homer's work and liked it, but he had never really looked at it seriously. Here was his chance. What he saw on this day drew him in, pulled at him somehow. He was impressed by the artist's "The Army of the Potomac—a Sharpshooter on Picket Duty", "Winter—a Skating Scene", the beautiful "Kissing the Moon" that reminded him of Hokusai, the seascape "Moonlight", the "Fox Hunt", and the "Searchlight on Harbor Entrance". An hour went swiftly by and his appreciation for Homer grew and grew.

Finally he was looking at Homer's "Dad's Coming". Something about it really grabbed him. The horizon at Gloucester harbor ran straight through the very center of the painting. Three sailboats appear on the horizon, on the left, barely distinguishable. Two more appear closer to shore on the right, but are not the focus of attention. On the far right a fishing net hangs on a rack to dry. Attention centers on three people, two children and their mother, or maybe their older sister.

Slightly to the left sits a young boy of eight or nine in a straw hat on the prow of a beached dinghy. The boy is looking at a tiny sailboat on the horizon at the far left. Presumably it is his father returning. Dominating the left side of the painting is a young woman holding a little blond girl of about five. The child is looking over her mother's, or sister's, shoulder toward the fishing net to the right.

But it was the figure of the young woman that really caught his eye. She is slim, though not as slim as the anorexic fashion models of today. She is looking neither at the little boy nor what is presumably her husband's, or father's, boat on the horizon but at the shore behind the boy. What is she thinking about?

What really got to Harry was the young woman's face. She didn't appear old enough to be the mother of these children. And her face. Though partially hidden by the head of the little girl, her face was not only beautiful, it was quite unlike the face of any nineteenth century woman whose portrait or photograph he had ever seen. Somehow it was a face from today, from the present. Who is she? What is she? What is she thinking? Is she relieved that her husband, or father, is returning safely from the sea? Is she thinking of anything at all? She seemed as enigmatic as the Mona Lisa.

He stared at the painting, at her, for a very long time, oblivious to all the other patrons strolling behind him. He lost track of time.

Slowly there awakened in his mind the memory of one of Akira Kurosawa's last films, "Dreams", a two-hour affair composed of eight unconnected dream episodes. One was about a little boy wandering in a forest and seeing a procession of people costumed as foxes going to the "Foxes' Wedding". Another was a beautiful segment about a very strange procession through the "Village of the Water Mills". A third was about a Japanese army officer veteran encountering a parade of the ghosts of the men he had led into a fatal battle.

But the episode of the film that came to mind now as he stood looking at the Homer painting was the one about Van Gogh. A young Japanese painter is strolling through a gallery of paintings by Van Gogh. He pauses and studies one of them, "The Bridge at Arles". In the foreground is a group of women washing clothes on rocks by the river. In the background is an arched stone bridge.

The artist stares at the painting for a while and suddenly you realize that he is "in" the painting. He can hear the gurgling of the river and watch the women scrubbing clothes on the rocks. He walks down the bank to them and asks, "S'il vous plaît , madame, ou est Monsieur Van Gogh?" The woman nearest him points to the distance and replies, "Il est là, monsieur."

So the painter, artist's kit under his arm, sets out to find Van Gogh. He passes through real villages and scenery that you recognize in Van Gogh paintings and even passes through large-as-life cardboard cutouts of trees and houses from other Van Gogh paintings. Finally he comes to a field of golden grain on a hillside. Not far from the top of the hill is Van Gogh, bandaged ear and all, working away furiously at a canvas on his easel. The Japanese painter approaches him to ask him something. Van Gogh, played by Martin Scorsese, who helped finance the film, mutters something, grabs up his easel, canvas, and brushes, and hurries away over the top of the hill.

As Van Gogh vanishes over the crest of the hill, a flock of crows suddenly takes flight from the field of golden grain. Almost instantly we see the Japanese painter back in the gallery looking at Van Gogh's painting "Crows", which is identical to the scene we had just seen in the film. End of episode.

Harry stood looking at the young woman in the Homer painting. He lost track of time and couldn't put out of his mind that if he concentrated and wished hard enough he might be able to step into the Homer painting and back in time and talk to the beautiful young woman. The stirring inside him told him he was in love – with a woman in a painting over a hundred years ago. He knew it was crazy but that didn't alter its feeling of reality.

Slowly he became aware of a gentle sea breeze on his face and warm sun on his skin. He found himself standing on the shore looking at the ocean to his left, a low grass-covered embankment to his right, and straight ahead, about thirty yards away, the little boy sitting on the boat, the young woman, the little girl, and the fishing net. He hesitated for a few moments, felt his pulse race, and then began to walk slowly toward them. The little boy saw him first but didn't say anything. The young woman, beautiful without makeup, looked up at him and smiled and the little girl turned her head to see what was going on.

Harry stopped. He was sweating in the breeze. He didn't know what to do or say. He managed to stammer "Hullo. Who . . . ? What . . ." He choked up.

The young woman looked at him, smiled, and said "hello."

Then . . .

Appendix V

Religion Exercises Influence in US Political Decisions

Just for the hell of it, let's end this book with an interview by journalist Gloria Paiva published on 29 October 2006 in newspapers in Brazil's four largest cities, Rio de Janeiro, Sao Paulo, Minas Gerais, and Brazilia. My translation from the Portuguese follows.

Religião exerce influéncia nas decisões políticas nos EUA

Nas decisões políticas norte-americanas, outro elemento mostra sua força: a religião. O partido republicano é composto, em sua maioria, por politicos declaradamente protestantes.

Especialmente nos Estados do sul e do meio-oeste, tópicos como o aborto e os direitos dos homossexuais são temas de peso na hora de votar.

Nos EUA, quase todas as 50 constituições estaduais dizem que "deve existir uma barreira entre a lgreja e o Estado". Mas, principalmente nos Estados que pediam a separação do pais na Guerra Civil, isso não ocorre nos pleitos.

Segundo o presidente da associação Americans for Religious Liberty, Edd Doerr, a divisão regional das tendências não é em vão. "A população desses Estados é, predominantemente, protestante e conservandora", analisa.

Para elas, os direitos dos homossexuais, o aborto e mesmo as aulas de ciências (ondo há polêmica sobre o ensiono da evolução humana) são fatores importantes politicamente.

Na sextra-feira, o próprio George W. Bush disse que a "instituição sagrada" do casamento deve ser preservada (entre homens e mulheres). Até o ex-premiê da Alemanha, Gerhard Schroeder, expressou, em livro recém-lançado, sua preocupação com as fortes manifestações de fé cristã do presidente norte-americano.

In North American political decisions, another element has shown its force: religion. The Republican Party is composed in its majority of people who are declared Protestants.

Especially in the states of the South and Midwest, topics such as abortion and gay rights are important themes at the ballot box.

In the USA almost all of the 50 state constitutions state that "there shall be a separation between church and state." Moreover, it is mainly in the states that tried to separate from the US during the Civil War that problems are occurring.

According to the president of the association Americans for Religious Liberty, Edd Doerr, the regional division of these tendencies is not in vain. "The population of these states is predominantly Protestant and conservative," he notes. For these gay rights, abortion, and even teaching evolution in science classes are politically important factors.

On Friday, George W. Bush himself said that the "sacred institution" of marriage must be preserved (between men and women). Former German Chancellor Gerhard Schroeder wrote in his recently published book his concern about the strong manifestations of faith of the American president.

Books by Edd Doerr

Min liv som Humanist (My Life as a Humanist) (2004)

Rejoyce! Rejoyce! (poetry) (2004)

Somebody Has to Say It (2004)

Great Quotations on Religious Freedom (with Albert J. Menendez) (1991, 2002)

The Case Against Charitable Choice (2001) (with Albert J. Menendez)

Six Stories and Seventy Poems (2001)

Cómo Mantener la Cordura en un Mundo Loco (Spanish translation by Herenia and Edd Doerr of Sherwin Wine's *Staying Sane in a Crazy World*) (2000)

Vox Populi: Letters to the Editor (1999)

Timely and Timeless: The Wisdom of E. Burdette Backus (Editor) (1998)

The Woodcutter's Tale, illustrated by Michael Hauck (graphic stories) (1996)

The Case Against School Vouchers (with Albert J. Menendez and John M. Swomley) (1995)

Religious Liberty and the State Constitutions (with Albert J. Menendez) (1993)

Catholic Schools: The Facts (1993, 2000)

Dancing on the Wall (poetry) (1993)

Religion and Public Education: Common Sense and the Law (with Albert J. Menendez) (1991)

Church Schools and Public Money: The Politics of Parochiaid (with Albert J. Menendez) (1991)

Images (poetry) (1991)

Abortion Rights and Fetal 'Personhood' (with James W. Prescott) (1989, 1990)

Religious Liberty in Crisis (1988)

A Hitch in Time and Other Tales (fiction) (1988)

Dear Editor (1988)

Parochiaid and the Law (1975)

Eden II (fiction) (1974)

The Conspiracy That Failed (1968)